Live True
From Fear to Freedom

By

Dr. Donna Kiel

Live True: From Fear to Freedom

As You Wish Publishing, LLC

Connect@asyouwishpublishing.com

ISBN-13: 978-1-951131-45-6

Library of Congress Control Number: 2022903420

Printed in the United States of America.

Nothing in this book or any affiliations with this book is a substitute for medical or psychological help. If you need help please seek it.

TABLE OF CONTENTS

INTRODUCTION

"It is better to live your own destiny imperfectly than to live an imitation of somebody else's life with perfection."

— Bhagavad Gita

I began and finished writing this book just 30 days before the news of the global pandemic began to infiltrate our world. As divine intervention would have it, my brilliant publisher had sent the book back to me asking me to make some changes. I started the changes just as our country went into lockdown. Rather than throw myself into writing, or even baking sour dough, I threw myself into anxiety and attempted to navigate the ongoing uncertainty.

I avoided the book for the two years of the pandemic. And then, once again, my brilliant publisher gave me a deadline for submission. I had to submit now or risk starting over. Honestly, I couldn't endure one more something being taken away. The pandemic had taken so much away and seemed never-ending. I needed something to make sense, and I needed to be in control of one thing—this book.

Everything that happens to you, happens for you. The submission deadline looming over me was prompting me to emerge from the self-imposed quarantine of writing and to emerge to refine this story with new truths and new discoveries learned during the time of lockdown and beyond.

Pre-pandemic, this book was intended to provide a road map to finding the truth that infuses life with meaning, purpose and joy. During the pandemic, I consumed myself with researching and learning about the brain, anxiety, and how we can deeply connect with our own lives. The lack of connection with the outer world created a bright spotlight on the need to connect with our own inner world. In that process of learning about the brain and connection to self and others, my world was transformed and changed in glorious ways. What you will see in this book is a true journey of truth. It is when you find the pathway to your true self that you emerge not only living true but living with peace, purpose, and true meaning.

Within the pages of this book, I share the research and insights I have gained in my role as a researcher, a coach, and a teacher. My quest to find my true self, to understand my own fear and anxiety, and to be what I thought was the best version of myself led me to become a researcher, coach, and teacher. Ironically, it was the great pause of the pandemic that gave me clarity and insight.

This book is not about changing who you are or about finding the next best strategy to live your purpose. There are plenty of phenomenal books out there about that. This particular book is about my journey of uncovering those choices and living in truth. It is about discovering that your fear, your anxiety, your anger, and your sorrow are all incredible gifts to be celebrated, loved, and honored.

For decades I have been seeking solutions to those emotions that are uncomfortable and painful. I became a professor and researcher to discover the ways to make my

INTRODUCTION

life have less suffering and angst. I gathered along the way the skills of life coaching, counseling, and Emotional Freedom Techniques (tapping), meditation, and principles of neuroscience. All of that knowledge and expertise has been incredible and important. Yet, I kept searching. Nothing ever seemed to completely manage the angst, anxiety, anger or sorrow—until the pandemic.

In the silence of the pandemic, I discovered the brilliant truth of our brain. We are each equipped with this incredible brain that is powerful beyond measure. This glorious brain of ours with two hemispheres that include a cortex and amygdala in both hemispheres manages our thoughts and feelings in miraculous fashion. In a flash of an instant, I realized the truth—that the sorrow, anxiety, anger, and fear of our amygdala are something to be celebrated and cherished. There is nothing I needed to seek to fix that part of me. Everything was perfect and whole.

You, too, have within you all that you are seeking. You are capable of grace and anger, humility and pride, growth and determination. Living a truth that is uniquely your own and which elevates you to your highest self is your birthright and destiny. My challenge has been being able to hear the words that would speak my truth to my own stubborn searching for something else.

Could the truth of our life be as simple as what Glinda the good witch tells Dorothy in *The Wizard of Oz*? Could everything we are searching for be right here in our hearts? The answer is simple—yes. In this book, I share a formula to transform fear into peace that comes from living our truth—living true. The formula is:

FEAR + WATCHING + WANTING + WELCOMING + WONDERING = **PEACE**

Reflecting on my life, listening to my students, clients, and teachers, I have seen these four key choices ignite wisdom and meaning in life. Since I tend to easily forget details, I used words that start with "w" to make it easy to remember the choices. Whenever you are stuck and your body feels the pain of an untruth, whenever you feel like you cannot find answers or your keys, you can choose to watch, want, welcome, and wonder. Choosing each of these actions has been my source of truth and joy, and I hope the same for you. In this book, I will share how this simple four-step process can transform your life as it has mine. Here are the four steps and a summary of the key points.

Watch. There is a wisdom within you that is your unique superpower—you just need to see it. All we need to do is to watch. Just carefully become the observer of your own life and not the victim of circumstances or perpetrators.

If we can look and examine the moments of our life that have brought us the greatest joy, we are one step closer to the wisdom. Choosing to watch rather than to react can give you the clarity to see your life and your work through the eyes of your own inner wisdom. When we choose to watch, we ask ourselves what has brought me fear, what has brought me joy, and how do I move more toward joy?

INTRODUCTION

Want. Knowing what we want is the first step of trusting ourselves enough to make those wants achievable. We can become so busy or confused we become uncertain about what we want. When we don't know what we want, if we watch, and allow ourselves the quiet to be observers of our life, we can trust ourselves to pursue what we want.

Welcome. We all are afraid. We innately either want to fight the fear or flee as fast as possible away from that fear. There are only three fears that keep us from our destiny. The fears of abandonment, shame, and betrayal are all about disconnecting from the love that is our natural birthright. When we welcome whatever is happening to us with loving compassion, we can shift from a hopeless state of feeling trapped to becoming empowered with the limitless capacity to create.

Wonder. Quitting is the most underrated strength. The moment we want to quit whatever is happening because we are wondering what more there is or what might feel better, we are making the most powerful choice to live our life with truth. There are times when we need to wonder, take inventory, and wake to the things that are dimming the light of our brilliance.

I hope this book opens the door to peace to you. For as long as I remember, I have been searching for the better version of me and fearfully trying all the things that I thought could make me the *real* me. It took that long to discover there was nothing to search for and nothing to do. The truth, my truth, and your truth are that all we need and are right here inside of us. Each wonderful part of us is already perfect in every way. All we need to do is to take this hero's journey, notice the helpers along the way, and celebrate our unique perfection. If you are ready to truly experience the magic of your life, turn the page and sit back for the greatest ride ever!

WATCHING

CHAPTER 1 – MEETING CHOICES

"In everyone's life, at some time, our inner fire goes out. It
is then burst into flame by an encounter with another
human being. We should all be thankful for those people
who rekindle the inner spirit."
— Albert Schweitzer

I am searching for something I have not lost. This line
from the Talmud is the most accurate description of my
life. I have been on a tireless search for answers,
insights, and the wisdom to make meaning out of this life
of mine. I was under the mistaken impression that the
wisdom I was seeking would emerge from outside of my
mind and heart and could be found in research, in the lives
of everyone else but me, and of course, on social media. I
always felt I had lost something, or that perhaps I was the
lone human being born without clarity of who she is and
where she belongs.

The wonderful thing about constantly searching is that
eventually, you find some answers. Looking back on the
volumes of self-help books, the endless hours of *Oprah*
interviews I have watched, the workshops, and even my
own academic career, I have evidence that we humans are
these fact-finding, answer-seeking, problem-solving
machines. We are relentless in wanting more and wanting
to know stuff.

The greatest discovery for me has also been the evidence that every single one of us can produce the wisdom to have our best life. We all can produce wisdom with laser-like precision and with tremendous abundance. The definition of wisdom is the soundness of an action or decision with regard to the application of experience, knowledge, and good judgment. Wisdom is our birthright. We all have it. Wisdom is not something that is outside of you—it is right there under that furrowed brow trying to figure out what the heck I am saying.

Wisdom doesn't come magically without turning on that questioning machine inside you and setting the calibration to the right level. The key that turns on the machine of wisdom inside of each of us is *choice*.

Knowing we have choice is an entirely different matter. For me, in my darkest hours, my wisdom machine seemed broken and I couldn't find my choice or any choice. How we see our world and what meaning we give to what we see is the most important superpower of being human.

It was the last day of Day Camp, and only one of the nine-year-old girls in my group had not yet swum in the deep end of the pool. I was the camp counselor for eighteen girls in the nine-year-old group. I was thirteen, had just graduated eighth grade, and so, of course, I could be the leader of a group of nine-year-old girls given the vast years of my life experience. Leading nine-year-old girls was a cross between herding kittens and an episode of Housewives of Day Camp. At times, the girls would be playfully romping with each other, and one second later, there would be tears and stomping of feet. Now, with the last day of Day Camp, I was determined to have all the girls pass the swim benchmarks, which included swimming across the pool in deep water. Just one girl kept me from the goal.

Ariana (not her real name) had long dark hair that matched her dark skin. She was taller than the other girls and seemed older than nine. She always seemed to have her agenda each day but would eagerly do whatever I asked her to do. On this day, I enthusiastically said, "Ariana, it is your day to get your swim badge." She looked at me and said, "I'm not sure I can swim in the deep end." I confidently said, "I'll make sure you are okay. I'll be with you each step of the way. We will do it together. Okay?"

We both got to the edge of the deep end of the pool. I told her, "I'll get in first, and you jump in, and I'll catch you. We will start by the side and then move out." I said, "Ariana, I believe in you, and I know you can do it." She watched me get in and then jumped right in like I told her. With one arm on the edge of the pool, I grabbed her, and for a few moments, everything was great. I started to let go of her so she could start swimming across the pool. The moment I let go, she grabbed my hair and pushed me under. I tried to get loose of her grip but couldn't. I kept going deeper as she kept shoving me down. I pulled at her, and for a flash of a moment, we were face to face with only an inch separating us. I saw the most awful fear in her eyes and a painful look of betrayal that I will never forget. I went under, and this time, I couldn't get up. Everything went dark. I couldn't see. All of a sudden, I saw an image of my body in a casket with my family crying over me. Then something shifted. I felt a surge of water underneath me, and it lifted me back up to the surface. It felt as if there was a wave pushing me up. I felt an arm around my waist. A lifeguard was pulling both of us to the side of the pool.

That moment of going under for what felt like a final time was surreal. I had no control over my body. The world went dark, and I could no longer hear the yells of kids in the pool. My mind seemed to float away from my body. I saw this image of myself in a casket that felt real. Had I died? What was happening? A strange hush came over me. I heard the words "Wait—not now." I felt a force underneath me. The wave that lifted me made no sense. I was in a high school gym pool, not a lake or ocean. Perhaps it was a miracle. Perhaps it was my sheer will to survive. Perhaps it was both. All I know is that moment of impending death at thirteen changed me forever. At that moment, being rescued from the pool, I made a vow. I never wanted to be the cause of anyone feeling the depth of the fear that Ariana felt. I had betrayed her. She trusted me. I trusted myself, and I had no idea what I was doing. I could have killed this little nine-year-old girl whose parents had just sent her off in the morning to her last day of Day Camp.

Our life experiences are always giving us data from which we create choices. What keeps us from those choices is often our interpretation of what we believe to be true. The truths we create in our minds are not always accurate—most of the time, they are actually pretty inaccurate.

After the incident in the pool, the story I told myself was that I caused Ariana's fear. I was the perpetrator of a moment in the pool that could have killed us both. I labeled myself as unworthy and selfish. I believed it was my need to have each camper reach the goal of achieving a swimming badge that put her life at risk.

Finally, at fifty-nine and in therapy, I located the key to turn on that darn wisdom machine of mine that had been dormant. I had held that story of that day at the pool so secretly with shame and fear. I had never told anyone that I felt I was this terrible fraud who almost killed a kid. As I told the story of thirteen-year-old me without any swim lessons myself teaching a nine-year-old to swim, my therapist kept saying, "What?" I had not even seen the absurdity of the situation.

There is a glorious moment when you find something that was always right in front of you. You feel both stupid and brilliant. I had to be introduced to the fact that I had this inner wisdom waiting for me. I also had to be introduced to the choices that would make the wisdom have clarity and meaning. Meeting choice with the confidence that you have all you need inside of you can shift your life. Really believing you have choice requires compassion, kindness, an open heart, and the belief that you are a complicated and preciously complex being worthy of being loved. In the moment, you can let go of the mistaken notion that you need something other than your own self—you can really find the truth.

Keeping Choice in Sight

Right now, right at this moment, you believe something awful about yourself that is not true. Right now, there is something you want to fix about yourself, something you want to change because you think it is not right. Right now, there are judgments you believe are factually true, and that is just not right. They do not support you or bring you to your highest potential. I had a hard time learning to question the awful things I believed to be true about me. I kept losing the damn key to the wisdom machine.

A righteous truth is one that emerges from a sense of goodness and justice. A righteous truth about you is the only truth worth listening to because righteous truth knows you are good, whole, and complete, just as you are. That moment in the pool began a journey of not trusting myself and not believing I was worthy. I was my harshest judge and critic. I tried so hard to fit in and make up for being the selfish woman I saw myself as.

The great thing about losing your keys in general or losing the knowledge that you have choice is that people always want to help you find them—both the keys and the choices. The typical first question is, where were you when you had them last? I usually respond with, "I have no idea."

We easily forget that last moment we felt we had choice the same way we forget where we had our keys. The key to keeping choice in view is to pay attention to the people who are nudging you toward finding it. The nudges don't always feel so good. As a matter of fact, the nudges to finding your choice often feel like hurt, pain, and suffering.

CHAPTER 1 | MEETING CHOICES

I had such a moment of suffering as I read a group text in which I was the topic. I had mistakenly been added to the group in a way that feels like God's hand of destiny and the cruelty of technology. I read the words, "That b***h thinks she can have it all." I felt the intensity of shame flood my body. I wanted to disappear. The "having it all" being referenced in the text was my attempt to join in with this group of women who opposed my lifestyle choices.

I had been the good girl who sought the approval of friends, family, colleagues and even the Starbucks barista. In a desperate search to find anywhere where I could fit in, I wanted to fit in everywhere. For over five decades, I believed fitting in happened when you did everything for everyone else. The sacrifice to be what other people like is the loss of your wisdom and truth. When you choose others first, you lose trust in yourself.

The moment a woman stops listening to the voices saying she should be what everyone else wants her to be, she locates that choice that turns on the force for her to become the powerful person who can unite this world. My first reaction to the text saying that I can't have it all was to beg for forgiveness, to create lies that would get me back into the good graces of the group and somehow cast away the judgment of others that I was unworthy. But something happened this time. This time, I closed my phone and cried. I did not respond. Somewhere in the depths of my soul was desperation for freedom from a truth that was not right. More than fitting in with this group of women, I wanted freedom from the struggle it was for me to pretend that I belonged with them.

Here's the thing—you can have it all—and there is no reason to deny the truth of who you are or what you want to fit the definition of life that comes from someone else. On the day of that text, I chose not to respond, not apologize, not get angry, not be hurt, and to step into the truth. I did believe I could have it all. I believe we can all have it all—whatever that means. I had spent years lying to myself about my worth, and in turn, I had to lie to others about what I wanted. I did want it all, and I wanted to be happy and to have my life have the meaning and impact it was meant to have. I wanted to find and use my choice to have the life I wanted.

Your Choices Not Their Choices

Choice can be so darn confusing. Often, we think we have a choice when really it is someone else's choice. I wanted a new life, not for the sake of pleasing someone else but for the sake of finally making myself happy. I wanted a life that was my creation and not a version of someone else's list of what my life should be like. I also wanted the safety and security of my job in education, my family home, and a circle of friends who had seen me through all the muck of life. I wanted it all. During this moment of truth of wanting a new life, I was also completing my doctorate in educational leadership. I was researching the leadership skills that inspire schools to change and grow. I had a very successful tenure as principal of a school, and my dissertation studies were an ethnographic study about my leadership.

CHAPTER 1 | MEETING CHOICES

I dove into research on theories of change and culture. I poured over my journal notes as principal, studying my own life and responses. My autoethnographic research was turning into an opportunity to carefully examine who I was and who I wanted to be. I was uncovering the truth of the way I sabotaged my happiness. I stopped fighting reasons to get into therapy and found a great therapist.

My doctoral research, my time in therapy, my unending reading of self-help were making me wildly anxious. I felt like I was in an endless game of hide and seek. I would discover the key to leading change in a school and feel like I was losing myself. I had an endless bank of questions about my life and what to do to make the pain stop.

I was an award-winning, work-obsessed professional who received accolades for being tirelessly dedicated. I was efficient and creative. I was depleted and detached. I believed I had to sacrifice happiness in the short term to achieve success in the long term. I had been raised to believe that the harder I worked, the more value I had. I was thriving in a work culture that allowed work to extend well beyond the workday. Technology made me accessible all day and night. Being principal felt like being an educator, therapist, mother, father, and friend. I was overwhelmed, and I was losing myself to my labels. The label of the principal had me mistakenly feeling that I was immune from feeling isolated and alone. The label of academic had me mistakenly feeling answers were within someone else's words. I was defining my life by what I did rather than who I was.

I found that I wasn't alone in the cycle of work-driven success as the things that defined my life. Whenever I would ask friends how they were doing, their response was the same as my own—busy. They were busy and tired. They were tired and busy. We were all racing through life feeling as if there was no other choice.

I started to observe my friends and my students. I started noticing what challenges people were bringing to me. There appeared to be an epidemic of women who were suffering from the illness of perceived success. I didn't know what to call this strange disease I was seeing, so I started naming it "the wanting more phenomenon." I found seven common symptoms of wanting more:

1. Success
2. Exhaustion
3. Guilt
4. Anxiety
5. Longing
6. Anger
7. Detachment

Each symptom was directly related to a very successful life—which is weird to think that success was causing us to feel so unhappy. Our schedules that honored hard work at all costs were exhausting us. Our inability to have enough time to give attention to the things that matter or even give time to the things that didn't matter left us feeling guilty. Our endless to-do lists and trying to keep up a social media façade of happiness caused anxiety and panic. And we seemed to share a longing to have all of this be different. I found that our tone with each other about work was marked by words of busy, angry exchanges and endless to-do lists. I was angry that I couldn't handle more work. I was angry I had no time for myself. I also found that to cope, I detached. I pretended that yoga was my centering time just for me when in reality, I would get lost in yoga to detach myself from feeling emotions and rather feel the awful pain of being bent like a pretzel. My friends did everything from drinking to dieting and binge-watching Netflix shows. I was seeing in everyone around me the imposter that I was becoming.

In November of 2017, I sent a Thanksgiving message of gratitude to a client for her collaboration on a project we were doing together. Part of the text was ass-kissing, and part was genuine gratitude that she trusted me to do this important work. Her reply made time stand still. She said that there was a quote that captured what she felt about working with me. She shared the Albert Schweitzer quote about rekindling the inner spirit of another once the flame has gone out. I read it over and over again. I felt the indescribable feeling of freedom that comes from truth. It was as if she had seen inside my soul and offered the most authentic words to the question that plagued me and became increasingly hard to hide.

She went on to say that I had ignited a passion in her and that I was an incredibly creative and inspiring force in her life. I sought words of praise like a hungry lion seeking her next meal. And while I craved acceptance and accolades from others, these words felt different. It didn't matter to me that she was praising me; what mattered was that the Schweitzer quote captured the connection between the two of us.

This was a different message of gratitude. As a professor, I knew my students often said my classes touched their hearts and changed their life. I dismissed their comments as ass-kissing to get good grades. I was not a rigorous and challenging academic, but students always said I was kind and inspirational. I dismissed that as my high need to be liked and accepted along with getting praise. It was easy for me to find my countless faults and disregard affirmations. But this message was different. The words felt like my own and felt like hers—there was no separation between her and me.

I realized the text wasn't about me; my client was seeing herself in me. Our connection had opened a door for her to reignite her passion. Our connection mattered—to her and now me. The connection was my key to choice.

My acceptance of her, even though she could be a pain in the butt at times, and my acceptance of myself sparked that purpose that was uniquely hers and uniquely my own. In that brief moment of a text, there was a clue to who I am meant to be.

That text tasted like truth and felt like freedom. I was gathering evidence that I had been creating an inaccurate interpretation. Fear of shame, abandonment, and betrayal had become the lens through which I was seeing the world. I couldn't see that the text saying that I couldn't have it all was a truth that was a testimony to my creativity and compassion. I was seeing my life as the good girl who was failing at being good. I had been raised to be the good

Catholic girl who believed following the rules of culture and groups was the only way to go to heaven and to gain love and affection. Being a good girl is an anxious, exhausting, and painful role to play. That text from my client awakened the question of what more there is in my life. This life, filled with culturally appealing success, was filled with guilt, shame, and longing, and I wanted more.

I started a training program to become a life coach. During a practice coaching session, I said out loud, "You don't need to be a good girl anymore; you just need to do good things." I was speaking to myself. I was being coached through my latest panic attack. When I thought of the critical email that had launched this most recent panic, I felt pain in my chest, and the muscles of my arms were weak, and my hands were sweating. I had always been the good girl who did the right thing and who would people-please her way to gaining positive strokes. Usually, if I made a mistake, apologizing and fixing it made me feel better. Not this time.

Your body tells you the truth about the choices you have in front of you. My body was telling me that my apologizing and blaming myself for doing something wrong was not the truth. Each time I thought about the email and the request from my boss to fix things, my body would tense. I couldn't eat. I couldn't sleep. I had believed my panic attack was the result of my fear of getting fired. I became desperate to make sure I did everything I needed to do to honor his request. Each thought sent my body into a frenzy of lack of appetite and pain.

In the coaching training session, my colleague asked me, "What do you want to happen?" I thought I wanted to be left alone. My colleague asked me again, "What do you want to happen next?" Something shifted this time when she asked. I wanted to be believed. I wanted the sender of the email to not abandon me. My coach then asked me what I thought the email was saying about me. I believed his email was saying that I was defective and should be cast away.

In coaching, we would use *The Work of Byron Katie* as a process of inquiry to examine limiting beliefs such as mine. The process involved looking at the belief and asking, is it true, is it really true, who do I become when I believe it is true, and who would I be without the belief that this is true? As I was coached through the questions asking me if what I believed was true and all the other questions, I went along with the process.

The answers to the questions were like breadcrumbs leading me on a path to find the choice I needed and wanted to make to step into my own wisdom. I had made up stories in my mind that had me interpreting every difficult moment of longing to belong as an indictment of my worth. No one needed to tell me I wasn't worthy; I did that all by myself. I had silenced the wisdom of what made me happy and the brilliance that was my destiny.

Truth is a feeling we have in our body in the same way we feel fear. Our minds can try to distract us, but that state of happiness is felt in the reaction of the heart, the stomach, and every other part. As a researcher, a teacher, a principal, and a professor, I was always seeking solutions to my pain

16

and suffering. I wanted the latest theory or research to tell me the next best process to get through the day. When I would read the research or go to self-help workshops, I would jump for joy if someone's story sounded somewhat similar to mine. I'd immediately adopt whatever practice they would use to my own life, thinking that this would solve my dilemma. The process seemed logical, methodical, and it worked—for a little while at least.

I have this wonderful retired friend who says to me often, "I just want the absolute answer to how to live a happy life." I wanted those answers as well. I had mistakenly convinced myself that 1) something was wrong with me that needed to be fixed, 2) I don't need anyone but me to succeed in this world, and belonging is not the priority, and 3) there was one answer that would solve suffering once and for all.

Here are three things that you need to know more than anything else—and things I need to remind myself of each day. **First, you are not broken and do not need to be fixed, and you haven't lost anything. Second, you have a powerful capacity to grow and evolve.** In other words, the clues to what will ease your suffering change as you change. Each day you are a new you, and each day, there are new challenges and new learnings—until you die—if you're lucky. **Third, you are a brilliant problem-solving machine who already has found solutions in your life and who can figure out anything.** Our main job is to connect and to always be researchers of our own life, seeking out the clues that will uncover the choices that can set us free to reach our highest and truest potential. We get all confused about our independence to live our unique calling and our natural dependence on each other. It truly is far better to live your destiny imperfectly rather than live someone else's perfectly. The only way to get to your own destiny is by walking alongside another who can welcome you home to you.

CHAPTER 2 - HELLO WISDOM

"Live as if you were to die tomorrow. Learn as if you were
to live forever."
— Mahatma Gandhi

O n the first night of class, I always ask my graduate
students to answer the question, who am I, without
using any labels, including their name. Every time
I do this, I am amazed at how difficult it is for the students
to introduce themselves without a label that puts them in a
category or group. I am a professor, a mom, a grandma—
but who am I really? What is the essence of my true being?
Who is the real person who shows up when I feel afraid, or
a friend is hurting? It is difficult to get to that description
without examining your life.

I know it sounds trite, but there really is only one you.
You are a unique expression of all the goodness of
humankind and all the not-so-goodness of humankind—and
so am I. I've come to believe that we can start to recognize
that goodness by examining the defining moments of our
life. I don't mean telling horror stories of our trauma, but I
mean looking at the moments of our life in which we
became the hero of our own journey.

When I ask my students to share the response to who
am I, they come up with great descriptors like I am kind,
loving, scared. Since I always want to know more and I
want them to really know more, I ask them to imagine they

are watching themselves the very first time they remember being scared. I ask them to tell the story of that moment.

There is a great power in telling the stories that have been rumbling around in your head as if you were watching a movie happen. Somehow, this more observer role takes away the stuckness in our trauma or our fear.

In examining my own life, the first time I felt afraid was on a cool fall night in October of 1965 as I sat in the back seat of my parents' 1964 Buick. The car was parked on a typical Chicago side street. I was left alone in the car to wait for my parents, who were inside the home visiting my new baby brother, Roger. For months before, I had excitedly awaited the day when I would become a big sister—my first purpose. I would be a big sister who would teach my younger sibling to play. I would be the big sister who so gently took careful care of her dolls and now could take careful care of a real baby.

The day of my brother's birth is forever memorialized in my first-grade school picture. On picture day at the Catholic school I attended, you could wear any dress outfit of your choice. On picture day, my mom was giving birth to my brother, and so my father got me ready for school. In that first-grade picture, I am wearing my snappy school uniform, and my hair is combed like a little boy. I look happily adorable. This is the only school picture that I like, as what I see is a bright-eyed, blonde, clean and cute kid.

My brother Roger was born with Down Syndrome. In 1965, it was typical for parents to be advised to place Down Syndrome children in institutions. At the time, the medical advice was thought to be the compassionate solution that would keep the parents from suffering the sorrow of watching their child die. Back in the 1960s, the life expectancy for Down Syndrome children was a few years.

My parents, in general, were very compliant people who thought anyone in authority was automatically right. As devout Catholics, they were rule followers and fearful. Growing up Catholic, there was always some gloom and doom fear that launched a cavalcade of votive candle lighting and saying rosaries. Roger's birth began a lifetime of special prayers for him.

Roger was placed in a foster home for special needs babies immediately following his release from the hospital. He never came home to the nursery my parents created for him. There was never a big announcement of the birth of the baby boy for Fran and Harry and his big sister, Donna, and big brother, Tom. Instead, there was a secret late-night visit to the foster home where he was beginning his life.

I sat in the dark in the back seat in an instinctual silent stillness that something was wrong. I don't recall asking any questions or anyone explaining to me what was happening. The mood was heavy with sadness. My parents seemed to be different people than I had known. I know I was afraid. I remember wanting to disappear.

When my mom finally came back to the car, her tears and silence deepened the new feeling of uncertainty and fear that were growing in me like a raging wave about to drown my little body. My mother's sorrow was a confusing call to action for my six-year-old self. I wanted to help. I wanted to stop the tears and make it all better. I could feel the physical pain of my mother moving away from me.

I was losing her. I had lost the dream of a baby brother, and she had lost the dream of a son. I could feel my mother's pain, and I wanted to make it go away. I believed she needed me to be a good girl and to be quiet. That moment in that back seat, watching the mother I loved and adored slip into the river of the sorrow of a dream dying was awakening the purpose of my life. I went from a playful child to a quiet, hidden and good little girl.

My mom was this brilliant contradiction of unbounded joy and intense anxiety. Before Roger's birth, she was this vibrant, loving, and funny presence in my life. My mother was one of eight children of Polish immigrant parents. My mother's family was a loud, energetic, deeply connected tribe of hard-working, WWII, depression-surviving characters. There were five girls and three boys in the family. My mother was the second youngest sister. My mother adored my grandmother, who never spoke English but who could convey love and affection that consumed me with joy. My grandmother was a large woman who would scoop me up into her lap and hug me in a way that said I was special and safe.

My grandmother lived with us for a time before Roger was born. I remember my mother would lay with me until I fell asleep at night. My mom would sing me this song that I think she made up. The lyrics were "goodnight, sweet Jesus, keep us at rest, goodnight sweet Jesus, goodnight." I can still remember my mother cuddling me as she sang. I also remember my grandmother calling my mother's name in Polish, "Franya, Franya." My mom would jump up and run to her. My mom was a loving and devoted daughter— she was teaching me that love. I wanted to be just like my mom. That compassion has been with me ever since. Watch your own story and tell it as the observer. Who are you? Who is that hero who faced fear for the first time?

Using Worry

For me, examining the past stories of my life generates the same worry and angst I felt during that moment. I even feel the exact same tightness in my body. There is so much data for our path in life and work in what we chose to worry about and how we responded to worry. We worry about that which we cannot control, but that same worry can create amazing skills that can propel you to success in work. As you are examining your life like you are watching a movie, looking for that first moment of fear, also look for what you worried about. My worries have become some of my best skills.

At fifteen, I worked a part-time job on Saturdays cleaning the offices of the trucking company where my father was the accountant. I had to go to the offices each Saturday at 4:00 a.m. before the weekend shift would arrive. The offices were more like desks located just adjacent to a truck dock. Each desk was filthy with soot from the trucks. I hated the job, but I had been working since I was twelve, and this job paid a decent five dollars. My mother would drive me to the trucking company and wait for me at one of the desks. I'd clean the offices, and we would go home.

Saturday, January 11, 1974, was a very typical Chicago winter day, with a temperature that was below zero. When my mother and I arrived at the office, we went to the door which was locked with a padlock. Our usual practice was for me to take the key and unlock the padlock. This day, the lock wouldn't budge. My mother tried. I tried again, and nothing would unlock that lock. After what felt like hours of trying, we gave up and decided to go home.

When we got home, my dad was sitting on the edge of his bed in his bedroom, which was just adjacent to our kitchen. My mom went toward him as I got my coat off. I started in the room to hear my mom scream asking, "What's wrong?" My father was pale white and having a hard time breathing. My mom was panicking, saying, "Let's call an ambulance." My dad had always been a forceful presence. He said, "NO. NO. NO." He couldn't breathe, and my mother couldn't function. She was crying and kept saying, "Oh my God, Harry, oh my God."

My dad said, "Drive me to the hospital." My mother started to cry. She got quiet and sobbed. I said, "I'll drive." I had never driven before. I took charge and told my mom to get in the back seat with my dad. I could drive to the hospital. Ironically, that afternoon was my first driver education class behind the wheel.

We got to the hospital. My father was whisked away, and I sat with my mother, praying a rosary. She was frantically breathing heavy and sobbing. What felt like hours went by. My mother was in the bathroom when a nurse came out and asked if we wanted to see my dad. I went into the room and saw my father, who looked far worse. He was lying on a table, and his color matched the white sheets. I went over to him, placed my hand on his arm, and said, "I love you, Dad." He looked at me and said, "Take care of your mother."

The nurse asked me to go back and wait. As time went by, I held my mother and prayed with her. I was filled with fear and with compassionate calm. My charge was clear; I was to take care of my mother. The doctor brought my mother and me back into an office. He started by saying my father was a lucky man. His heart had stopped beating just as the doctor was passing by his room. The doctor was able to revive him. He was alive, and that is all that mattered.

Worry motivated me to take charge and drive my dad to the hospital. I was afraid, I was worried, and I had to do something. There are times when we must choose to worry because our ego, which is our call to action, needs to show up. If I had chosen to just compassionately listen to my father's resistance to getting help and his prideful disdain of an ambulance, he would have died. Find that worry that has created in you a superpower. For me, I became a leader, a doer, a woman of great conviction and determination.

There is a tendency for culture to shame women as worriers—especially moms. But worry for me has motivated research, action, and decisiveness. Watch your life with the eyes of someone who loves you, who trusts that you have all you need, and who can see that uniqueness that is already there.

CHAPTER 3 - YOU WIN

Wanting to succeed creates confusion for women. Winning is confusing as well. Too often, women feel ashamed to want more, to be the center, to be the one to succeed. Women who celebrate success with enthusiasm are often branded as boasting ego maniacs.

We mistakenly believe that wanting more is the opposite of selflessness and service. To be clear, there are two types of wanting. The wanting that gives very temporary ego-centered joy and satisfaction—like wanting that delicious chocolate. Which, by the way, is not bad. Then there is the wanting to succeed that reaches to your very soul and is a craving you cannot avoid. It is the wanting of success that gives life meaning—a life of joy, a life of love, and to have your life matter and have a positive impact—that is true wanting. When we silence the wanting of more of that, we crush our wisdom and we deny our dreams. The challenge for me has often been naming what success I want. If you can watch your life and ask what brought you joy and what made you feel that warm blanket of love that lifted your being to the greatest energy and happiness, you gain great data around how your wisdom and your wanting come together to create your purpose.

The first time I felt that joy of success was when I was eight. My brother, Roger, was placed in Misericordia Home for the Developmentally Disabled on Chicago's south side when he was a month old. Misericordia was a Catholic facility sponsored by the Sisters of Mercy. It opened in 1921 as a maternity hospital for women of "meager means," both wed and unwed. Then in 1954, Misericordia became a place to house young children with intellectual, developmental, and physical disabilities. Misericordia retained its mission to help unwed mothers by employing them to take care of the children. When I think of this now, it seems this rather odd contradiction of kindness and cruelty. Having pregnant single moms who needed financial assistance care for babies and children, many of whom would die, seems rather cruel.

Roger's care at Misericordia was nurturing and kind—at least that is what my mother told everyone. My mom would take me with her to visit Roger though I only got as far as the waiting room. I spent years in that waiting room. I passed the time by counting the ceiling tiles and trying not to stare at the children who would pass by with the young pregnant caretakers. I sat silently, listening as the aides would talk about the latest baby to die. I'd see parents leave crying. I sat alone as disfigured children and hydrocephalic babies with heads twice the size of their bodies were wheeled past me. And then there was Roger. Occasionally, my mom would bring Roger to the waiting room. He always smiled at me even though his body was often listless and weak. Each time I saw Roger, I felt this calm come over me. I remember thinking he was the most beautiful baby. He had big blue eyes and beautiful blond hair. He laughed all the time. His skin was soft, and when I was with him, I felt happy.

We celebrated Roger's first birthday at Misericordia. I have a picture of me holding him in front of his first birthday cake. He is smiling at his cake as I am holding him to blow out his candles. For decades, I looked at that picture and saw Roger's loving smile. Recently, I looked at the picture and saw a little girl who looked nothing like she did in her first-grade picture. Just one year later, the little girl in the picture holding her one-year-old brother had changed. At seven, I had dark circles under my eyes, and my haircut looked as if I had cut it myself, and I was fat. I can only imagine what that first year after Roger was born was like for my mother and father.

My mother and father found ways to cope. My mother would make friends with the unwed mothers who cared for Roger and distract herself by learning their tragic life stories. She would give them gifts that seemed like special bribes to take care of Roger. She would leave me sitting in the waiting room for hours, and she talked to each of the workers and the nuns who ran the place. My dad worked, drank, and became sullenly quiet. He never went with us to Misericordia, and I'm not sure why. Or at least I don't remember him going with us.

Misericordia became a haven for my mom and Roger. The word misericordia is Latin for mercy. Roger's joy the moment he saw me was the definition of mercy. He saw me, my soul, and I saw his. Roger, this Down Syndrome, culturally unacceptable being, became my first experience of triumphant success.

That first year of life, with our short visits, Roger and I formed a bond that defied disability or circumstance. Roger was grace. Roger was mercy. He was everything magical and good.

There is a magic about any baby. The smile and engagement that are without judgment are contagious and enlivening. Roger had that special quality of a normal baby, but he also had something different. Maybe it was his nonverbal cues and my silence that merged to create this special magical language of love, or maybe it was just our shared willingness to be there for each other. Whatever it was, Roger gave me confidence and a belief that I was special and had a secret power. I was his sister, and he loved me. Even if the world couldn't love this fat, shy kid, the Down Syndrome kid loved me.

When Roger was two, we began to bring him home for a few hours each Sunday. At two, he still didn't walk and was getting too heavy for me or anyone to cart around. No one seemed anxious to help him walk. After all, everyone was under the doctor's given assumption he would die soon. But Roger was far from being a frail child who would die. At eight, I was determinedly confident that I could teach him to walk. I wanted him to walk. I wanted to be the one to get him to walk. Keep in mind, I never had been around babies or children and didn't know anything about teaching.

I began this long and arduous process of propping Roger up, quickly moving about three feet from him and reaching out my arms to have him walk to me. Time after time, he would flop to the ground and smile at me to pick him up. And time after time, I would pick him up and smile. I kept at it. Finally, I decided to move across the room where it would be hard for me to get to Roger quickly. I propped him up, walked across the room and as I turned with my arms outstretched, he was there—laughing

30

as he walked into my arms. One Sunday afternoon, I taught my brother to walk. I didn't teach my Down Syndrome brother—I taught the brother I loved and who loved me. I was a success. I was a teacher. I was confident.

Our memories of fear easily consume us and become the prominent stories of our lives. But the moments of our fear and other successes are the greatest data that can give us direction for our life path. The blissful joy and triumphant success I felt when Roger walked was a clear indicator of my passion to teach, my passion to lead, and of my ability for patient compassion. I wasn't just successful; who I was can be described as a woman of determination, kindness, and power. I wanted him to walk, and I wanted to be the one.

When I think of that moment of Roger walking all on his own to my outstretched arms, there is a blissful joy that consumes my entire body. The feeling of love and happiness is like an electric wave of energy that awakens every cell of my body. There is a great deal of bio-cognitive research, especially that of Dr. Mario Martinez, that suggests there is a healing power in those moments of blissful joy for our bodies and our minds.

All I know is that when I think of that moment, I feel empowered, creative, brilliant, and strong. I've had the belief that my ability to connect with Roger in that unique way was easily transferred to any child. I seemed to have a natural knack for making children smile and feel at ease.

When in your life have you experienced a blissful joy that consumed your entire being? What happened at that moment? The memory of that moment is a choice available to you whenever you need it.

At a Martha Beck workshop, she described a similar phenomenon as "dropping into love." Very similarly, Martha talked about her experiences as an expert witness during a contentious legal trial. The attorney questioning her was attacking and aggressive. Martha dropped into this state of love, and in her mind, she said, "I love you, and you love me." She then shared how the attorney backed down and became almost complacent in his questioning. The energy of love she had dropped herself into was radiating out to the attorney, and he was absorbing that same love.

At the same Martha Beck workshop in which she described the positive impact of dropping into love on the field of energy that you project in the world, Martha shared the way this energy could transform matter. She would take a strong, metal spoon, drop into the moment of love that was in her mind and bend the spoon as if it were butter.

I wanted to bend a spoon. I wanted that feeling of bliss and peace that I knew was somewhere deep within the memory of teaching Roger to walk and other memories of blissful joy and connection. For me, the love that Martha described had happened in moments with my children and with Roger. Martha told us to pick a moment that would allow us to drop into love and then hold the spoon while we dropped back into that memory then bend. It didn't work. I tried again. It didn't work—again and again.

After the workshop, in the quiet of my own home, I closed my eyes and pictured my daughter at three months old snuggled up next to me softly sleeping—this was heavenly love. I reached for the spoon, and it bent as if it were soft rubber. I chose another spoon and another—each one bent more easily than the one before. The memory of the bliss of the love of my daughter filled my entire being, and the energy was powerful. Why could my memory summon energy sometimes and not at all times? Our thoughts are powerful tricksters in our lives. With the direction of Martha Beck, following her instructions, I couldn't bend the spoon. When I dropped into that moment I wanted so much, the moment of love with Roger and my daughter, those moments of bliss, spoon after spoon would bend with ease.

Our thoughts are powerful. Our thoughts and memories can liberate the truth of who we are, or they can keep us trapped in a lesser version of our self. Your dreams and your potential live within the memories and thoughts you hold in your mind, and their power comes to life when you choose to be a woman who wants, a woman of wisdom—your truest self.

Gather the memories of wanting and winning that have defined your life. We spend so much time musing over the tragedies, which is often healing, but we need to find those moments of bliss and ask how we can get more of that. As an adult woman, I tend to be serious, thoughtful, and studious. After all, I am a professor, and I try to fit into that costume and play the role. The truth of any of our lives is that getting through any challenge is not about the roles we play but about the inner joy we have experienced. If we can get back to that spark of joy, we can find what we need to face any heinous moment.

Growing up, I spent my days playing on the city block in Chicago where we lived. The block was filled with lots of kids around my age. One of our favorite play activities was to line up and race each other down the block. We would get in a horizontal line with our toes on the crack in the sidewalk. One of us would get the honor of saying, "Ready, set, go." We would all race to the middle of the block, which was my house. The first one to reach the sidewalk crack in front of my house would win. I won all the time. I remember feeling as if no one could ever beat me. I was fast, confident, and triumphant, and I had two best friends. Steven was two years younger than me, and Carol was my age. I knew I could win the race every single time, but something in me wanted them to win and to be proud too.

I remember standing at the starting line, launching into my unbeatable pace and slowing down. First, I let Carol win. She jumped around and told her mom about her conquest. I had to now find a way to let Steven win. He was smaller and didn't have the height to outpace Carol. At five, I was pretty crafty. I remember putting one foot in front of Carol as we started. She tripped, and I recovered to get back in the race. I kept pace with Steven until the last three feet and fell back so he would win. Despite Carol saying the race was unfair, the look of pride and joy on Steven's face sparked joy in my heart. I had the confidence I could win the race, but when I could share winning with Steven and Carol, I felt bliss. To me, the true winning was in the joy I could see within my friends.

Harvard professor Jerome Kagan noted that along with our competitive nature and survival tendency for aggression or violence, there is an even stronger biological bias for kindness, compassion, and love. Heroic moments of compassion and selfless acts during World War II or other heinous times prove the human capacity for sacrifice to be kind and loving to others. We can mistake kindness as enabling or people-pleasing—I know I did.

I want others to be happy. I am a card-carrying people-pleaser. While I love making other people happy, I also criticize myself for being a people-pleaser. I bought into all the supposed women's empowerment material that said we should take care of ourselves first and stop people-pleasing. I couldn't access the joyful bliss of winning because I believed the untruth that I was just a people-pleasing weak woman. I was trapped by how I interpreted the messages of culture.

People-pleasing and kindness are not self-harming, nor are they bad things. You read that right. It is time to stop believing that people-pleasing women are weak and disempowered. We may just be following an internal wisdom to be kind and our path to true success that comes from uplifting others. The key to authentic people-pleasing that does not compromise one's agency in this world is making sure it is what you want.

Taking time to ask, "What do I want?" and then ask again, "What do I really want?" is extremely vital to finding the truth that gives you the life and work you want. The body will give you a signal of what you want, and your stories will tell you what you want. Examine what brings you joy and what brings you sorrow. Look at the difference in what those two opposites bring out in you. Listen to your voice of who you are and your unique wisdom. It is absolutely okay to want more, to feel unsettled, to tap into the truth that is longing to break free. Listen to the unsettled voice, the longing, the quiet that is in you.

We humans are wonderful, magical and predictable beings. We give ourselves clues that something inside of us is shifting towards our truth. In my life, I started to notice that when a friend or family member was stepping toward a new relationship or was choosing their own wisdom, they would start to buy new clothes, change their hairstyle, paint a room, or get new furniture. It's as if we are clearing the past away, with the new stuff as a flag, saying, I'm different now. That is running right into the truth!

WANTING

CHAPTER 4 - TRUSTING YOU

"Our labour preserves us from three great evils—weariness,
vice, and want."
— Voltaire, Candide

The greatest moment of a woman's life is when she realizes she can choose to honor herself. It is the glorious happening when her desires are not diminished or shamed and when her wants are welcomed with freedom. Women have a legacy of ancestors who denied their dreams to survive. Women of our past had to play small and keep quiet so as to not be shunned or even killed. That legacy of the good girl is one that will take centuries to undo—but every woman deserves the freedom to choose her true self.

For me, that great moment of honor whispers every so often. I may not be there yet, but there are times when the heavy burden of denying my own wants and needs becomes exhausting, and I am able to say, damn it. Those moments are gloriously light and joyful. We can make the choice to want and to honor who we are.

For me, that moment came when a wave of emotion filled my body as I stood in the middle of my kitchen. It was just a typical Saturday filled with mundane tasks of grocery shopping, meal prepping for the week, yoga class, cleaning, and then perhaps I'd squeeze in writing the book that would transform the world. I started that day like I do every day. Before meditation, I would write my desires for my life—sort of a mix of practical goals and inspirational reminders that, at close to sixty, I wasn't done yet. I write what I'm grateful for and then my intentions for the day. The intentions were always the same and always seemed just a bit out of reach. I intend to be loving, kind, and present.

I had asked Siri to play a random shuffle of Melissa Etheridge's songs. Just as I asked myself the task-orientated, what now I heard were the words of this Melissa Etheridge song:

> *She's got her sweet children*
> *She's got her home she's got some land*
> *Her earthly possessions*
> *She's got a ring upon her hand*
> *She tried to be a good girl*
> *She tried to make everything right*
> *She tried to kill the voices*
> *That haunt her each and every night*
>
> *She looks up to heaven*
> *And wonders why love is so cruel*
> *She loves him, won't hurt him*
> *Can't stop the wanting of you*

The words and the music filled every part of my body with an explosive force. Uncontrollable tears flowed from the depths of my heart. My entire body began to move and dance. The lines, "she loves him, won't hurt him, can't stop the wanting of you," echoed in my heart and mind.

Something was happening to me. Melissa Etheridge's brilliant lyrics were announcing a call. The words felt like truth, "She tried to be a good girl. She tried to make everything right. She tried to kill the voices. That haunt her each and every night."

I had created a life in which I moved so fast, did so much, worked so hard that the wanting in me was silenced. How did I get here? Why would I want anything but what I had? I was the epitome of success: I had a nice home, a family I adored, amazing friends, fancy job titles, and a doctorate. And I wanted something more. At that moment, with Melissa Etheridge's strong and powerful voice echoing in my soul, I fell to my knees. How had I lost what I wanted most? I wanted myself. I wanted to love me, to feel comfortable in my skin, to walk into a room with the grace of knowing I was okay just as I am.

This time what I wanted was not a degree, a paycheck, a thing. This time what I wanted felt more important and more confusing. I wanted me. I wanted to know what I wanted and to fiercely live with honor, loyalty, and commitment to myself. I wanted to stop being the good girl who did everything she thought she should. I wanted to show up for me. I wanted to have my own back when times get tough. I wanted. I wanted.

What began in my kitchen on a typical Saturday morning was a visit to my truth. I was not the good girl, or the professor, or the mom, or the grandma, or any label that I slapped on myself to try to fit in. I didn't want it all anymore. I didn't know what I wanted, but this was not enough. The haunting voices in my head were saying, "Is this all that there is?" No, I wanted more.

The problem was I didn't know what more I wanted. I didn't know how to let go of the habitual quest to succeed, to fit in, to win goal after goal. I had lost myself to the busyness of my own life. I had been trying to fix myself for as long as I could remember, and it had served me well. Wanting to do more, be more, and give more had accomplished so much good in the world and had given me a pretty awesome life.

Yet, day after day, I was growing in feeling anxious and unsettled. I would feel enormous shame when I made any sort of mistake. I felt like a liar and a fraud pretending to be a competent, skilled, and loving woman. Who was I, and what the hell was this longing?

I realized as busy as I was distracting myself from the calling in my heart, I had also forgotten the moment's clarity that led me here. Was there a moment of clarity in which I felt the peaceful assurance that this was exactly what I wanted? There was. I knew that feeling. I had to trace back that moment of wanting that seemed easier when I was twenty.

"That" wanting

At twenty years old, my priorities were getting through the last year of college without having to do any public speaking, laughing my way through working my part-time job at Sears Roebuck with the friends I had made, and figuring out my life. Like most twenty-year-old women in the 1980s, I had tried on all sorts of different ways to figure myself out. I wandered the path of dating, drinking, marching for women's rights, and changing majors in college. I started college with my mother's encouragement to be a chemistry major since I had won first place in my high school science fair. My tenure as a chemistry major lasted exactly one quarter. I sat in my first calculus class feeling like an alien being who could never learn this language and stopped that right away. I then switched to business as a major because my best friend at the time was majoring in business. We parted ways, and that major ended. There were more majors along the way until I finally landed where it felt like I belonged with a major in psychology. Psychology seemed to serve the need to impress people when I said it was my major, while also giving me actual time to try to figure myself out by learning the principles of the human condition.

In a moment at the kitchen counter of my parent's home, as I was talking on the phone to my then-boyfriend, who would become my husband, I had a moment of clarity. I have never forgotten the feeling of freedom—that was rare for me. He and I were having one of those meaningful life conversations of what we wanted next in between dancing around our wants and desires. He was clear on not wanting marriage or commitment. He loved his independence and wanted to travel the country. He also was head over heels in love with me, and I knew that. My voice rose from a place I had never experienced before. With calm conviction, I said, "I want to be a mom. I want to have children, and I want that soon."

I felt an urgency to have a baby since my mother told me that Roger's Down Syndrome may have been due in part because of her advanced age. She was over forty when she had Roger. Something deep inside my soul was speaking. For the first time in my life as an adult, what I wanted had nothing to do with pleasing anyone else. I wanted to be a mom. I must be a mom. This wasn't a choice; this was a mandate written in my soul. This wanting was my destiny. I could feel it in every ounce of my being.

At that moment, at the kitchen counter, talking on the phone, I felt I was with me. I also felt confident and calm. I knew I would have a child. I knew she would be beautiful. I loved her before she was even conceived. I knew her name. I knew her smile. I could feel it, see it, taste the truth of love in every ounce of my body.

The day my daughter was born, my heart filled with the greatest love I have ever known. As I looked at her, I felt as if I had known her my entire life. There was magic in that moment and every moment with her since then. I feel no greater truth that I was meant for loving my daughter and my son. Being a mom wasn't about wanting that label or that role in life. Being a mother, for me, was about celebrating the calling of my soul. I belonged here as a mom. I listened to the wanting in my heart. I wanted my way to the most meaningful experience of my lifetime as a mother of two people I admire and adore.

Now, approaching sixty, as I was in my kitchen listening to Melissa Etheridge, that clarity of wanting was missing. I knew there was something more I wanted, but I had no idea what that meant. Wanting doesn't always come to us with a loud announcement. What we want is often a whisper or, in my case, moments of anxious fear that were becoming increasingly paralyzing.

There was another stanza in that Melissa Etheridge song that not only stopped me in my tracks but felt like a call to action that I could no longer deny:

Keeping her desire paralyzed
She catches in the corner of her eyes
Tank top, smooth skin, soft lips, tanned thighs
How the hell's this ache ever gonna die
And we make our choices
Doing what we think is good
We deny our own dreams
Cause we think we've been told we should
We think we've been told we should

I could not keep the desire in me paralyzed. What was this desire? I didn't want the next goal, the next relationship, the next thing—I want me. I want to stop being afraid. I want to stop believing I am anything but good, kind, loving, and complexly human. I want to be okay with being vulnerable and honest. I want to follow the rules and break the rules whenever it feels right. I want to be alone, and I want to belong wherever I choose. I want me. I want to love and be there for myself. I want to celebrate all the parts of me that are the wounded and the warrior, the wise and the worrier. I want the unexpected truth that I am absolutely precious. I want that for me, and I want that for you.

Each day I realize the beauty and goodness in the people around me. I see in my daughter and my son the brilliance of their creativity, kindness, and humor. I see in my family and friends unparalleled acceptance and forgiveness. I see in my students care and striving for connections that matter. Each beautiful quality I can see in everyone else is only possible because each of those qualities exists in me. When I hold my granddaughter and am filled with indescribable hope and love for her beauty, grace, and love, it is because each of those qualities lives in me. When you find the moment of *that* wanting that defies denial, the wanting that will not leave you alone, and then when you choose to listen to that wanting, you are choosing yourself, and you are living the life that is your destiny. Whether that wanting is a job, a moment of success at work, to lead a meeting or to sit back, your life and your work need you to show up, choose you—hear your voice and silence the voices that say you are less than precious.

Finding the Want

I am an introverted, sensitive, feeling-centered, and often judgmental person. I judge myself and live in my own head so much that I often cannot hear the voice of truth.

So many times in my life, I have had no idea of what I wanted. I couldn't find it. I would so easily get lost in what might look good or what other people wanted. I would constantly ask other people, "What do you think I should do?" I wanted someone, anyone, to tell me what I wanted, and then I could try to feel if it felt right. I was great at making lists of pros and cons for any life decision. I would research, ask, try to feel, and wait.

What do you want? My coach, who I had paid, was yelling at me. She had asked me what I wanted, and I kept saying, "I don't want to feel this way anymore. I don't want to be anxious and filled with fear each day when I wake up." Her reply was consistent, "But what do you want?" She got louder and increasingly impatient. Now I wanted to make her happy and have her stop asking me what I wanted.

I kept saying my entire body hurts. I'm so scared that I can't even think. I am a fraud and liar in my own life. I want to have everyone believe me and leave me alone. She told me to stop, just feel that pain and focus on it without trying to figure it out. Why would I want to feel this suffocating anxiety? I had a hard time just focusing. I wanted to analyze the pain, put it in a box, and I wanted her to give me some inspirational message that would say I was alright. She patiently waited. She kept saying, "Stay with it; the feelings will go away if you just stay there and feel it." She was right—at least for a moment.

Then, she did it again. "What is it that you want? I want to know what you want." I used every eloquent phrasing I could to describe I wanted to be a woman who was not a crazy mess all the time. She stopped me. Why would I be so critical and demeaning to me? Why did I believe that I was anything less than a typical human? She asked me,

"What if you are absolutely all of those things and more? What if you are a liar and a fraud, and you are also brilliant and strong?" She went on to say that we are all liars and frauds and brilliant and creative. We are all good girls and bad girls. She asked me to do an exercise that answered the prompt, "If I were a lying con artist, I would—" fill in the blank. She wanted me to make a list of all I would do as a lying con artist. A day later, when I tried the exercise, I couldn't do it. The exercise itself paralyzed me with anxiety. I emailed her to tell her this didn't work. She asked that we speak again right away. She said she wondered what I was thinking.

I described the feelings of fear that rose in my heart as I attempted to describe what I would do if I were a lying con artist. I told her that it felt too real. I felt like I was confirming that I was indeed a lying con artist who didn't deserve my own life. She stopped me and asked me to share examples of what I created that the liar in me would do. As I shared those, her reply stopped me. She said, "What's wrong with that?" She asked me if I had ever read the poem "The Guest House." I had not heard of it before and asked if she could send it to me. I read the words and again had that moment of clarity.

The Guest House
By Rumi

This being human is a guest house.
Every morning a new arrival.

A joy, a depression, a meanness,
some momentary awareness comes
as an unexpected visitor.

Welcome and entertain them all!
Even if they're a crowd of sorrows,
who violently sweep your house
empty of its furniture,
still treat each guest honorably.
He may be clearing you out
for some new delight.

The dark thought, the shame, the malice,
meet them at the door laughing,
and invite them in.

Be grateful for whoever comes,
because each has been sent
as a guide from beyond.

    I wanted to welcome me home. Without a pause, I said to my coach, "I want to write. I want to coach. I want me. I want to welcome every part of me with love, laughter, surprise, and awe." She then said, "It is all about choice.

You can give yourself choices. You can choose to be a good girl, or you can choose to be the liar and the fraud. Each part of you is a choice."

There comes a time in a woman's battle to make it through this world when she realizes that every single part of her are soldiers that deserve honor, respect, and value. I want that choice to welcome all of me home. I want to open my door of resistance to say to that anxious and fearful woman who blames me for every misstep, "Hello, come on in, you must be exhausted." I want to welcome the woman who judges every single person and is so hateful. I want to laugh and say, "You've been working overtime." I want to welcome the compassionate, loving, beautiful woman who protected her mother, who adored her children, who inspired her students and who, after sixty years, still wants to make the world a better place. I want to welcome every part of me that wants and doesn't know what she wants.

CHAPTER 5 - LISTENING TO YOU

"Darkness cannot drive out darkness: only light can do that.
Hate cannot drive out hate: only love can do that."
— Martin Luther King Jr.

When I feel my body pull me away, I know it is time to listen. Our bodies are far wiser and far more in tune than our minds. Our bodies tense whenever there is an untruth about our goodness or our brilliance. Our bodies ease when we align with love and truth. It is the words we put on things that attempt to silence the clarity of our bodies. Choosing to listen to what you want allows you to liberate your body to be the brilliant teacher it is trying to be.

It was Roger who taught me the power of listening to my own body and voice. Roger believed he could do anything. We are the ones who labeled him with Down Syndrome and put him in a box of limitations, but Roger didn't have a box. I'm not sure if my parents ever considered giving up on Roger or stopping the rituals of visits. I wonder now if they ever fought with each other about the stress of driving back and forth to Misericordia to see him. I'm sure they had a choice. They could have done as many parents of Down Syndrome children did in the 1960s and let the state take care of him. They could have walked away. Being the parent of a different child had to be frightening. The shame and guilt had to be consuming.

At six, I was ashamed of Roger. I never talked about my brother to friends or at school. I do recall making up a story about Roger as a normal kid. My love for Roger was this confusing secret that I kept to myself. It was easy to forget the quiet, shy, good girl who was Roger's sister. I easily faded away. But Roger wouldn't allow it.

No matter how much I tried to forget that I had a Down Syndrome brother who lived in a home with frightening-looking other kids, the moment I would visit Roger, love filled my heart, and Roger's mercy welcomed me home just as I am.

Roger modeled this amazing confidence and determination. As Roger grew into a young adult, so did his joy. For years, I quietly watched Roger continually walk into any situation with an air of certainty. He approached any situation with a can-do attitude that would annoy and often embarrass me. He'd get into a car and say, "I drive," and then laugh. He believed he could drive or fly or work on my computer. He just assumed he could. He never doubted himself for a second. He seemed to know things or believed he knew things. Though he was mostly non-verbal, he had a few phrases that he would often speak. One of his favorites was to repeat my name with this laughing disdain as if he were saying, "You poor thing; you and your doctorate just don't have a clue." Of course, he would always smile most lovingly.

From the time I was six, I watched Roger enter any unknown, high-stakes situation with secure confidence. Along the way, I somehow absorbed Roger's air of egoless strength and his ability to listen to his heart that said that he could do anything. It was perhaps the greatest gift to my professional and personal life. I just always believed I'd figure out whatever I needed to figure out, and it would all be okay.

When I was 21, with introversion in high gear and self-doubt dominating, I answered an ad for a job as a school counselor. On the day of the interview, I arrived 30 minutes early and pulled my car over on a side street to wait. My heart pounded, and my face was turning that wonderful shade of red that pronounces, 'I am a chicken shit.'

Two weeks earlier, I had begun my first full-time job as a customer service manager for a mortgage company. A pretty impressive accomplishment for someone who earned only marginal grades in college and who, after changing majors 12 times, ended up with a bachelor's degree in psychology. Psychology as a major seemed to be a cost-effective way to manage my anxiety. Getting a full-time job would be my stamp of credibility.

On my first day as a customer service manager, I was escorted to a cubicle, given a binder, and instructed to read. I sat dumbfounded. The world of work was not what I envisioned. As I pretended to read the pages, I heard this whisper, "Get out."

Something was happening. There was an illogical and socially unacceptable whisper telling me to run away. I was this responsible, rule-following, good girl who always did what she was told. Now I was obsessed with violating the rules and jumping out of the window. As soon as the clock struck noon, I bolted. I raced to my car and drove away, never to return. I had failed.

Two weeks later, I sat in my car hyperventilating, waiting to interview for this school counselor job. I was filled with shame, doubt, fear, hope, ambition, and a dream for something I could feel but not articulate. My needy, good girl wanted to be hired to redeem myself. But something else was also happening. There was something mystical moving me forward. I'm not sure why I ever thought I could be a school counselor. I had never trained for the profession. Honestly, none of that qualification malarkey even crossed my mind when I called about the job.

On the visor of my car was a small card about 2 inches long and 1 inch wide. It had a picture of St. Jude, the patron saint of lost causes, on the front and a prayer on the back. While I was raised Catholic, my devotion was more in line with seeing prayer as the emergency red button connecting me to some higher power when all my lower powers were freaking me out. My mother, the real Catholic. She was the kind that would light votive candles, go to Mass each week, and say rosaries. She was also anxious all the time and afraid of everything. She wasn't exactly the best model of the calming and manifesting power of prayer. But on this day, I needed something—so bring on the prayer. For me, praying is this magical thinking that I am not in control of what comes out of my mouth, but rather God will take over and give me wonderfully articulate words that I speak without knowing where they came from.

The prayer on the card said, "Most holy Apostle, Saint Jude Thaddeus, I place myself in your care. Help me know that I need not face my troubles alone. Please give me courage in my fear, and healing amid my suffering. Ask our loving Lord to fill me with the grace to accept whatever may lie ahead for me." I read the card aloud—which was weird. Not only was I sitting alone in my car, now I was praying out loud. When I spoke the words, "Fill me with the grace to accept whatever may lie ahead for me," I felt this overwhelming wave of peace, calm, and love wash over me. Something happened at that moment. My entire world shifted. I was at ease, and the red flush of my face faded, my hands stopped shaking, and I knew. I had no idea why I felt calm, but I knew I belonged in that school.

At that moment, in my car, with a holy card, I found something that I had seen so many times in my brother Roger. I found a warrior who lived inside of me. I felt this loving-kindness for this scared, confused, strange little girl that was me who ran away all the time. I was her warrior of compassion. I welcomed her home and knew she had the courage and grace to handle anything. After all, she knew when to run away and when to get there early (even if she looked like a crazy stalker on a side street).

My choice was to be that warrior of kindness as I walked into that interview. Whatever happened, I was in a relentless quest to be the compassionate person I had become in each story of my life. The unexpected truth that compassion was the weapon that could fight away fear, self-doubt, and the delusion that I needed to be anyone except who I am had arrived. I chose to be that warrior of kindness.

I was hired as a school counselor in an all-girl private school. The job and the school became a haven for me to hone my skill as a professional and as a woman coming into her superpower of compassion. In that school, I would have some of the most joyful experiences of my professional life, and I had the most humiliating and humbling moments. Through it all, that prayer of St. Jude resonated in my heart, "Fill me with the grace to accept whatever lies ahead." I listened to me—to the me that said, "No matter what, I will be okay."

Not Listening

Our words can heal us, and our words torment us and can keep us from experiencing the life of joy that is our destiny. We can choose the truth of what those words have taught us about our resiliency and our strength, or we can get stuck believing we are defective or less than. I often would do both. Roger was in and out of my life each week. On Sunday, he would come home and fill my world with this unconditional love and simplicity. On Sunday evening, my mom and I would drive him back to the group home. Now, I wonder how I kept silent the words that worried if I, too, would be sent away on a Sunday night. The words surrounding Roger of *retarded, limited, unable* would fill my heart. I felt each word not only described him but described me. There are times when we need to choose to not listen to words to find that wisdom. Roger's own ability to fend off words was my model. I wanted to be someone that no one would give away.

After ten years as a counselor, I was asked to become the assistant principal. As a counselor, I found the formula to always engage the school leadership while also having an ardent commitment to working for the students. It was my devout loyalty and admiration to the principal that motivated me to take on the challenge. At the all-girl high school, I found the home that I needed to grow into my voice and power. The principal of the school was a woman I deeply admired and who, in many ways, stepped in as a mother, mentor, and friend. She offered me acceptance and spoke eloquently about the potential she saw in me. Besides that, she knew I was a hardworking, diligent, and dedicated worker.

I never felt complete confidence that I knew what I was doing as a school counselor, yet things seemed to work out well. My superpower was in connecting and empathizing with the girls—and protecting them. I was a vigilant counselor who would tirelessly work to help any young woman who had been wounded or abused. I fought child and family services for justice and worked hard to take care of our students. I had the great combination of dedication to perfectionism and fear of connection that resulted in an organized, effective counselor with great boundaries.

I was beyond excited when the principal asked me to be her assistant. It didn't matter that I had no training. I wasn't trained as a school counselor either. I loved the principal and would do anything for her. We became a pretty dynamic team. I always had her back, and she let me lie my way out of mistakes. I will always remember a meeting with her in which she asked me if I had done some task that was assigned to me. Typically, if I didn't do something, I'd find an excuse or a creative lie to cover it up. This time, I was tired, and my guard was down, and I just easily said, "Nope, didn't do it." She applauded my honesty and said,

"I wish you always felt you could be that honest." She didn't say it with anger or judgment but with a care that seemed to say she wanted to help me.

The racial slur scribbled on the bathroom wall in sharpie was a call to disciplinary action that I voraciously took on. No one was going to harm these young women with hateful words. No one would ever bring hate to this school on my watch. I became the mother lion protecting her cubs with tenacity and anger that was powerful.

I found out about the graffiti after school from our maintenance man, who was paying attention to the girls talking in the hallway. It was well after school had ended for the day, and basketball practice was happening in the gym. The maintenance guy went into the bathroom near the gym to see what the girls were talking about. Very smartly, he grabbed his digital camera (this was long before cell phones) and took a picture of it.

When he told me about it, I immediately said, "Get that down. Do whatever it takes to make sure no one has to see those hateful words." I ran down to the gym where the kids were and where the bathroom was. I had to protect those girls. I also had to know who did this.

I started to launch a typical high school assistant principal investigation of an incident. I asked kids what they saw, who found it, what was happening. The basketball team seemed to be the only ones around. I wanted to know who saw this. I could feel the humiliation, the shame, and the anger of anyone seeing the words.

The principal had been gone for the day. She often left school immediately after the last bell to take care of her elderly mom. She always supported our families and her own. As a Catholic school, she lived those values of faith and compassion. I called the principal's office and left her a voicemail knowing she often checked her voicemail in the evenings. Again, this was before cell phones and the limitless communication we have now.

I gathered as much information as I could and went home for the day. The next morning when I arrived at the school, there were parents of our African American students waiting for me in the hallway. At first, it was two moms and their daughters, then four, then six, then eight. I moved them all to a conference room.

I'd never witnessed the volume of agonizing pain, fear, and anger that filled that room. All I could do was listen and feel with them. They wanted answers. They wanted solutions. They wanted racial equality in this school, whose mission was peace and justice. And they wanted the principal.

In the mornings, the principal would arrive about an hour after school started so she could take care of her mother. I was there to cover, and I wanted to both do my job, protect her, and do the right thing. Each parent asked what we were going to do, and each parent asked for the principal.

The moment called forth every ounce of courage, calm, and compassion I could muster. I believed in the principal and knew she was a woman of integrity and justice. While the parents kept saying, "We know this is not you, it's her issue," I would not cave and said, "This is all our issue, and we are in this together." I also knew they were right. There needed to be an answer. There needed to be a strong response.

When the principal arrived, I quickly filled her in. The parents had stayed and waited for her. The meeting that ensued was the most awful experience of my thirty-year career in secondary education. The raw pain of the legacy of racial intolerance and hatred filled that room. There was nothing either of us could say. With each word, the parents got louder, more emphatic, and angrier. It was hours of demands and details that were not connected to the racial slurs being surfaced. Finally, the principal agreed to ongoing meetings and finding some solutions. I stood by her with loyalty and a commitment to support her and the school but also to follow my heart and values to fight against racism.

The next morning a student stopped me in the hallway to say that the entire school was going to stage a walkout at 10:00 a.m. that day. She asked me what would happen if she walked out with her classmates. Something happened to me at that moment. I looked into that girl's eyes which were filled with fear, and rage filled my heart. It was as if time stood still.

I wrapped my arm around the student's shoulder, and I said, I'll walk out with you. The student went on to say that the parents had called the media and were going to join. I told her to follow her heart and trust me that it would be okay. That moment offered me a choice. I was a loyal, devoted employee and admired my boss, the principal. I could choose to make this go away for her and tell the kid that everyone would get in trouble. She may have spread the word not to walk out. The other choice was to listen to my body that felt calm, strong, and loving. My body said, "I'll walk out with you—you are right."

After leaving the student, I ran to the principal and took charge. I told her what the school was planning and that I believed we should all walk out. I said, "The teachers needed to know so they too could walk out if they wanted to." There was a flurry of activity to get notes to the teachers telling them of the walkout. I could see television trucks pulling up outside my window.

At 10:00 a.m., one by one, in silence, all four hundred girls filed out of the school. The principal and I walked out together and stood with the girls. As I looked into the principal's eyes, I saw the depth of her pain and sorrow. The walkout, the racial slur, the anger of the parents had all happened under her watch. My heart ached for her.

The months and years that followed were always marked by that day of the response to racism and the memory of the words on that bathroom wall. The principal poured herself into finding ways to fight racism and intolerance. All the while, I knew that day with the parents changed her. She was afraid, she was uncertain, and she was someone I forever admire. There was a wounding by those words that was always beneath the surface.

Words are powerful. We have a choice as to which words we hear, how we hear them, and what they mean to us. After the racial incident, I chose to listen as my brother Roger did. I chose to listen to the unity of all the students who walked out together. I chose to listen to the words of parents who wanted equality for their daughters. I chose to listen to my own words of loyalty to the principal. I chose to listen to the words in my heart that said I was compassionate.

WELCOMING

CHAPTER 6 - SEEING YOU

"Your task is not to seek for love, but merely to seek and
find all the barriers within yourself that you have built
against it."
— Rumi

In our darkest moments, we sometimes cannot see the
brilliance of our own vulnerability and suffering. In
each moment of suffering is the gift of a call to action.
I have found that suffering, any form of suffering, whether
fear, anxiety, longing, or shame, is the inability to see the
love that resides in us. We have a choice within wanting to
want to see our truth. For me, seeing my own resiliency,
my own compassion, and my own kindness has required a
high-power magnifying glasses. The moments when I can
welcome the truth that is inside me, a truth that sees with
love and kindness, that is when the moment of *seeing me*
happens. In my life, moments of seeing typically start
somewhere in a muck of confusing tearful snot, like in
1999.

I had been the assistant principal for five years and had
been at the school for seventeen years, and I was an
emotional mess. I was about to turn forty, my daughter was
fifteen, and my son was twelve. My daughter was a
freshman at my school, which was hell for both of us. We
worked hard to both enjoy this odd connection between
mother and daughter and dodge each other throughout the
day. My daughter is a brilliant and wise woman. Despite

having her mother be the assistant principal, she forged her way at the school. I watched her join the tennis team, having never played an official game in her life. I witnessed her try out for the school play *The Miracle Worker* and be cast as the young Helen Keller. Her performance was astonishing. Putting aside my mother's love for her, what I saw in her portrayal was the depth of emotion, reality, and compelling wisdom that was Helen Keller. I knew it was difficult for my daughter to be at the school where her mother was charged with discipline and student schedule issues, but she had this way of kindness and compassion that gave me a safety net of loving acceptance.

At the same time that my daughter was thriving, my life was consumed with battling my raging demons of fear that said that I didn't belong anywhere. I felt like I was a failure as a wife, mother, and certainly as an assistant principal. My best friend at the time was a nun whose presence in my life was even more confusing. Everything felt chaotic and uncertain.

In April of 1999, an incident occurred at Columbine High School in Littleton, Colorado, in which two teens went on a shooting spree killing 13 people and wounding more than 20 others before turning their guns on themselves and committing suicide. Columbine put all high school administrators on edge. Schools began to draft crisis plans and talk about what to do with the threat of a shooting. None of that had been part of our world before Columbine.

In May, the principal went on a vacation with her family, leaving me in charge. The day the physical education teacher came to my office, I felt something odd—like something terrible was about to happen to me. The teacher shared that one of her students said, "Columbine could happen here. Anyone could bring a gun right into this school and do a Columbine." The teacher was visibly upset. I asked for details of what she heard, the name of the student and other students and launched right into assistant principal mode.

The very next thing I did was to call the principal. My call was both for my emotional support as it was to get her approval of what I was about to do. She listened and said to go ahead and talk to the kids and find out what happened.

The young woman who commented on Columbine sat in my office shaking. Before I even began to talk, she was crying. She said she knew she was in trouble, and she just couldn't get expelled. She said that this school was all she had, and she was just being stupid. She went on to share the details of her mother's impending divorce from her abusive father. She begged for forgiveness and to stay.

I met with her mom, who also cried a bucket of tears and shared her fear that her daughter would be expelled. The family was as broken and vulnerable as I was. I told them both that I needed to consult with the principal and asked that they trust me that we would do the best for the girl.

Every ounce of my being did not want to expel this young woman. She needed help; she did not need to be kicked out of school. When I talked to the principal, I explained in detail the emotional condition of the young woman and my theory that she was trying to get help. Her teachers described her as an outcast who craved attention. The girl needed therapy. The principal asked me what I was proposing as the action. I said, let's mandate her into therapy and then see if we can figure out how to have her back. Let's get a therapist's opinion about her stability and her ability to be at school. The principal agreed.

As I told the young woman that we would be requiring her to get therapy and then do what the therapist said, she hugged me and cried. I told her we needed the therapist to give us his or her professional opinion of her ability to be of no threat to herself or others. She and her mom eagerly agreed.

A week later, the principal returned to school and asked about the student. The student's therapist had released her to come to school. The principal looked at me with fear. "She cannot come back. You need to expel her." My entire body tensed, and my heart began to pound out of my chest. I felt my face turn a bright red.

I was angry. I was scared. I was ashamed. I couldn't do it. I couldn't expel this young woman. I carefully hid each feeling and told the principal I would follow through. My heart broke into a million pieces.

I called the student and her mom and broke the news that she was expelled, then fell to my knees in agony. What had my life become? Why couldn't I stand up for this young woman and myself? I told the principal I was struggling and needed time off. While she was supportive, she asked that I get therapy myself and that I allow her to verify this with my therapist. I knew I needed help, and so I complied.

The therapist I chose has been one that I had often referred our students to see. She was a social worker whose specialty was sexual abuse. The therapist had even seen the principal's daughter. I told my therapist that the principal wanted to verify my sessions and that she had my permission to inform her of my attendance in therapy.

What happened next remains one of the most vulnerable and painful moments of my life. I attended three therapy sessions and returned to work. I came back on a Saturday to catch up on details and ease my way back. I had materials to put in the principal's office adjacent to mine. I put my key in the door, walked into her office, and went to put the materials on her desk. On top of the desk was a legal pad with notes. In her perfect handwriting was my name, my therapist's name, the dates of my therapy sessions and more. With each line I read, I felt my body get weaker and shame flood my body. My therapist had shared the details of our sessions with the principal. In a flash, I imagined the principal telling my family and firing me. I wanted to die. The pain and shame were the most intense feeling I have ever had.

Something happened at that moment. There was a rage just under my shame that launched me into action. I jumped online and started searching for another job. I found an all-boys high school looking for a school counselor. I called, set up an interview, and started to clean out my office.

Monday morning, I had an interview with the principal of the all-boys high school. As I entered the interview, only

69

my second interview in eighteen years, I felt this energy to protect that little six-year-old who had again been violated by her uncle and the thirty-nine-year-old who had been violated by her mentor. I was passionate, articulate, and present. I wasn't the fearful, anxious assistant principal who cowered in the shadow of her mentor.

When I was asked why I was leaving a school I had been at for eighteen years, I easily responded that I wanted to go back to my calling to be a school counselor. I wanted to help kids to heal and help them to be successful. I imagined the young woman I had expelled. I wanted to fix this and to be someone who would have a positive impact. He hired me.

The words on the principal's legal pad said that I was someone who was not stable. I had worked for this woman for eighteen years, and I knew how her mind worked. I easily concluded she was about to fire me. I wouldn't let that happen. I couldn't. Something in me knew to get out and quit.

The principal asked to see me, which I knew was not good news. We never set up meetings with each other. I prepared my resignation letter and got the rest of my office cleaned out before the meeting.

As I entered her office, the principal guided me to the pink wing-backed chairs, which had a legacy of being the places where she had hard conversations. As we sat, she leaned in and said, I think we have a problem. She started to talk, and I said, "No, it is okay, there's no problem, here's my letter of resignation." I choose to honor me with kindness, gentleness, and loyalty to her.

Months after my resignation, I sent the principal a letter apologizing for anything that I may have done that was difficult. Old habits of self-doubt are very hard to quit. I don't regret sending her that letter though she never responded. Knowing what to quit and when to quit were things I learned from Roger—though, at the time, I didn't realize this was his lesson. Roger lived what I would learn was one of the four *freedoms of play*. I came across the four freedoms of play from a colleague at the university. She shared the concept developed by Scot Osterweil that defined the power of play to engage our minds and hearts because of the four freedoms that define play. The four freedoms of play include the freedom to experiment, the freedom to fail, the freedom to try on identities, and the freedom of effort.

Roger certainly lived each of the four freedoms, but the one that became aligned to his mantra was the freedom of effort. Roger was mostly non-verbal but had a phrase he loved to repeat. The phrase was "I quit." He didn't just say, "I quit." He would say, "I quit," and then laugh this rather snide laugh that seemed to say that he knew something the rest of us didn't. Roger lived his mantra. He would be the first to engage in any situation with energy and confidence, and then when he seemed to have had enough, he would quit.

One of my favorite moments of Roger's freedom of effort was during a hot Chicago summer. My mother had asked Roger to pull the weeds in the gangway between her house and the one next door (which would eventually become my house). My mom liked to keep Roger busy on his visits home, and Roger liked to complete tasks. On this day, my mother was being her usual pushy self and kept nagging at Roger to pull more weeds. He complied until it was time to quit. My mom, of course, did not think it was time to quit. She snapped at Roger and said, "Roger, pull those other weeds." My non-verbal, always compliant Down Syndrome brother looked lovingly at my mother, put down the weed puller and said, "F**k you." He laughed and went into the house. He was done. He quit. He wasn't angry. He wasn't wanting to put her in her place—though he did. He had the wisdom of knowing this was enough, and he could see his own goodness enough to welcome her into his world—as odd as that sounds—he welcomed her to truth.

When we can see our own goodness, when we can let go of the blame, the shame, the fear and know that we are born good, complete, and whole, then we can welcome ourselves to walk away when we need to and to walk toward when it is right.

The walking toward those who have wounded us is always so damn hard and so damn needed. I have never regretted walking toward anyone with love and compassion. I have tons of regret of walking away in anger. Being able to see ourselves and to consciously make the choice to step inside our own compassion takes the ability to know what to quit. The day I finally found the peace, the tenacity, the compassion to see myself and to quit seeing others as weapons to harm me, my world changed.

Ending the War

I never shared with my mother why I resigned or why I chose to work in an all-boys school after seventeen years in an all-women's school. I held that sort of vulnerable information like a shield that would not allow me to love her. I wouldn't let her see me, and in turn, I couldn't see me. The war that waged between us was polite, dutiful, and silent.

Then on October 30, 2003, I climbed the stairs I had climbed so many times before. As I walked into the bedroom I had called my own for so many years, I thought of the secrets and shame that had filled that room. I walked in. There she was. Her eyes were open, and her leg was hanging over the bed. The stillness in the room felt paralyzing. I reached over to touch her. She was cold. She was gone. She felt so cold. My mother was gone. I was numb. Here it was, the moment I had begged God to never have happened. Rosaries, votive candles, prayers, and wishes that she would always be here were dead. I feared her death, and I feared her alive. I had become artful at distancing myself emotionally from my mother in an attempt to guard my heart and to not have to experience this moment of loss. I failed in my attempt.

I looked at her lifeless and didn't know who I was. I reached over and took the curler out of her hair. She would not want the funeral home attendant to see her with a curler in her hair. Death has a way of moving you to do weird things like taking curlers out of someone's hair even though it wouldn't matter. I couldn't cry though I felt like I should. I touched her again. I fell to my knees. This voice surged up in me. Rest. Get some rest. It was the last thing my mother had said to me. Just the night before, she had called me. She was rambling on about getting a new television and shopping with my son. I was half-listening and mostly wanted to hang up. She said that I sounded tired, that I worked too hard. Her closing words were, "Goodnight, I love you, get some rest." Rest. All I wanted was to rest. Could this be happening? How could she be here and now gone?

My mother was a powerful force on this earth. Her personality and presence filled a room and also filled my heart. She was this amazingly intense contradiction. She was a determined, strong, and unbounded woman who lived valiantly through the depression and World War II and all the uncertainty that followed. She had three children, my older brother Tom who was thirteen years older than me, then me, and then Roger, born with Down Syndrome. She would describe my older brother's birth as the most frightening experience. He was born with an Rh blood factor issue and had to have a full blood transfusion. She often said, whenever my brother was difficult, that it was because of the transfusion, and we needed to be kind to him. Then she had me thirteen years later. The gap in time was enigmatic of something going on in their lives.

About five years before her death, I had taken my mother to my doctor when she was experiencing shortness of breath. My doctor was the leader of a famous hospital in Chicago and was considered the best in women's medicine. I wanted my mom to have the best medical care. During the office visit, the doctor calmly told my mom she was amid atrial fibrillation and would need to be hospitalized to reverse her heartbeat. The doctor's office was adjacent to the hospital, so we would take an elevator ride to the emergency room to get admitted.

The doctor was savvy enough to see my mom was prone to panic, and so she underplayed the event. We gathered up my mom and the nurse, and I wheeled her to the elevator. I chatted with my mom about getting her a silky nightgown and trashy novels to pass the time. I had lame attempts at humor about her saving an ambulance ride. At one point, the nurse turned to my mom and said, "You sure do have one special daughter."

Without missing a beat, my mom said, "Yes, having a daughter around turned out to be okay considering I never wanted her." I leaned across the wheelchair to see my mother's face. Did she just say she never wanted me? Could I push this chair through the elevator doors? So, she didn't want me, and then six years later, she gave birth to a Down Syndrome son that she was told to put in a home. She had one hell of a life. After my mom's heartbeat was normalized, I asked her about her comment. She said that she didn't want me. Her husband was an alcoholic, she had to take care of her mother, and life was hard. She didn't think she could handle a baby. And that was all. She never said, "But now I'm so glad." I wished she had said it.

My mom was a devout Catholic filled with fear and anxiety, believing votive candles and rosaries were essential to ward off any disaster. She would pray for everything. She would pray my father would keep his job, that his alcoholism would stop, and that she would have a happy death. I'm not sure what that means to have a happy death, but she prayed to die in her sleep—and she did.

As I stood in my childhood bedroom looking down at her still body, a wave of calm came over me. I adored my mother. I despised my mother. I desperately wanted her love and pride, and I wanted to both be like her and to be completely different. I was free now from that longing, or was I? She was dead, and now she could never give me the love I needed. How could I let go of the quest to earn her love that had consumed my driving ambition and life choices to be the good girl doing everything she thought she should do?

My entire life was a quest for my mother's love. The searching has taken me deep into the creation of secrets and lies that would consume me and persuade me that my life circumstances could be better. In that same bedroom where my mother died, she had found letters I had written to my first love. I kept the letters locked in a metal box. The lock evidently could be easily undone. I don't know why she chose to search my room, find the box and read those letters, but she did. I knew she did. At 15 years old, the violation of privacy was enraging to me and also humiliating. My mother had entered a world that I had kept secret—a world filled with shame and fear for me.

We never spoke about the letters. She never asked me any questions or offered any counsel. I did hear her talking to my aunt on the phone about me. She was wondering what was wrong with me and why I was violating Catholic teachings. She worried I would go to hell. I worried as well.

In that same bedroom, I had my first kiss and also thought about killing myself so many times. I was always pulled back by the Catholic teachings that said you would go to hell if you committed suicide. I was also pulled back by the deep love for my mom and dad and not wanting to cause them even more humiliation than I had already done. I gazed at my mother's brown eyes, the ones I had loved, and felt as if I had been released and also enlisted as the general in an army. I was in charge now. I was the boss. Her judgment, her criticism, her praise, her accolades were all gone now.

The strange feeling of calm and peace surrounded me as I stood with my mother for this final time. We were more alike than we were different. We were scared all the time, we loved deeply, and we wanted more.

My mother was a completely imperfect woman who was intense in every situation, and I craved her love. Could I ever embrace the truth that my mother was the center of my universe? She was more than just a woman who gave birth to me, and she didn't know how to love me. I didn't know how to love her. Now, how could I ever live without her and yet find that relationship with her that I deeply wanted and needed?

I held on to so many secrets as lame attempts to keep my mother's love. Now, I no longer was bound by the secret of the pain that filled our relationship, or was I? Like most mothers and daughters, she hurt me, and I hurt her. We were messy, imperfect, loving, and strong women who needed each other and who both stumbled through that need. After she died, the extra 90 pounds of weight I carried seemed to easily fall away and release the shame she and I felt. After she died, I was magically able to shed my fear of public speaking, and I became an expert public speaker, a school principal and eventually a coach and professor. Maybe all of that was because I was still trying to get her to love me.

A month after my mother died, I went away for a weekend. My relationship with my mother was a complicated, intense, unforgettable, and indescribable bond. I loved her, and I resisted her with an ardent defense that kept my heart hidden from her. Her death seemed to be the end of my lifelong habit of running away and running toward her. I wanted to be free, and I didn't want to let go. I wanted her to know me, and I wanted to know her. She was gone. The hope of that love was gone. As I was away for the weekend, I got my first tattoo. Impulsively, as is the truth with most tattoos of women of a certain age, I sat in the chair and handed the artist a napkin with the design. On the napkin was my mother's full name in script, and under her name, the words 'always in my heart.' At the time, I couldn't see that the act of tattooing my mother's name on my arm was inconsistent with the resistance, judgment, and anger I held toward her. Which was the truth? Did I love her, or did I despise her? I've battled that question as I've searched for the truth of who I am now and who I want to be. Love, and especially love between a mother and daughter, is a preciously confusing experience for us.

I had to quiet the fear, the longing, the expectations, the cultural demands of what a mother is supposed to be to quit the lie that my mother and I were broken. I couldn't quit her, and I couldn't quit me. I didn't want to. I wanted to quiet the interpretations of truth that she wasn't good enough, that I wasn't good enough, and that was all there is. In quieting the resistance, I would welcome the unexpected truth that what I wanted more than anything was to now create a relationship with my mother that was filled with grace for both of us.

My mother was gone, but our relationship would never die. I began to see me, and I began to see her with clarity. All the good in me and all the complex not so good was the same in her. I stopped fighting the choice to want my mother. She was my mother – the only one I would get. I wanted her love, and now I had the chance to create that love within me. When we choose to honor what we want – no matter how it ends up looking – we choose to see ourselves.

WONDERING

CHAPTER 7 - SEEING THEM

"Once we believe in ourselves, we can risk curiosity, wonder, spontaneous delight, or any experience that reveals the human spirit."
— E.E. Cummings

When we see the goodness, kindness, and beauty of another, we are really just seeing ourselves. When we see the ugliness and faults of another, we are also seeing ourselves. There is a wonderful Eastern spiritual belief called the Splendor of Recognition that says when the Divine created all the beings, human and nonhuman, the Divine hid part of itself within each. It is our job to recognize the splendor hidden with each being. I have found that when we cannot see this splendor, we cause ourselves incredible suffering.

We all have those people in our lives, present and past, who can just trigger us into a frenzy of thoughts and feelings that are paralyzing. For me, that person is often my mother—or people who represent my mother.

Those triggers have incredible power to remove us from our truest selves and turn us into wild beasts of anxiety and anger. While it may not seem possible, we can find our way out of those moments of triggering with the choice to welcome and recognize who is talking to us within our own head. That voice that says, "You're not good enough, you're a liar, you're not worth it," is not your authentic voice. It is the voice of all the past pain and suffering. It is also the greatest opportunity to shift—even if the shift involves kicking and screaming.

For a long time, I confused the voices of fear and self-doubt as my own. I had this incredible experience of shifting that belief—if only for a moment—when my son was six weeks old and in the hospital. We had brought him to the hospital because he had bloody diarrhea. I was a frantic and anxious mess. I was in the hospital room with him as the nurses attempted to put an IV in his tiny little arm. That didn't work, so they tried his head. The screaming got worse and worse with each attempt. My anxiety and fear grew as loud as his screams. The nurse looked at me as I held him and said, "I think you need to leave and let us try this without you." She ordered me to take a walk.

I reluctantly listened. I had thought I appeared calm, but the nurses knew the baby was absorbing my fear and my anxiety. My mother had met me at the hospital. She found me in the hallway as I began the walk. I explained what was happening with an agitated tone. I snapped and angrily said, "They're trying to get an IV, and they won't let me calm him. They sent me out here," and then I said with the harshest tone, "What do you want!" I was pissed. What did she want from me? I couldn't hold it together as I had done since I was six. I was a complete mess. She calmly said, "Nothing, I'm just here."

We began to walk down the hall. I pulled away from her, so there was a nice distance between us. I was angry, and she was the best and closest target. I couldn't control what was happening to my son, so instead, I would control the cruel way I handled my mother.

My legs felt like rubber, and I was shaking all over. My mother moved closer. She put her arm around me, and I cringed. My body had been so tense and so tight that her touch sent pain shooting through me.

Somewhere deep inside me, I knew my mother loved me. I loved my mother. I more than loved my mother; I adored my mother and had tried to earn her love since the day my brother was given away.

My mother didn't understand me, and I didn't understand her. She judged me, and I judged her. I knew she would do anything for me. I also knew she had the power to infuriate me and shut me down. My mom's words could cut right through me with a criticism that would knock me to the ground. My mom's selfless love could also lift me in a way that only a mother's love can provide. My way to cope with the unpredictability of our relationship was to distance myself emotionally. Whenever I was with my mother, I was a controlled, analytical, intellectual daughter with academic degrees far beyond my mother's high school diploma, and I was completely in charge. I knew what was best in any situation, and she knew nothing. I had convinced myself I was smarter and more competent than her. It was a lie that I told myself, so I wouldn't need her. I didn't want to need her. Needing my mother would mean if I lost her, there would be a tremendous pain. It was all illogical and completely consuming. My entire coping mechanism was the result of made up of stories and interpretations filled with shame, abandonment, and betrayal.

My mom walked beside me down the hospital hallway. We walked back and forth and could hear my son screaming. She tried again to reach out to me. She put her arm around my shoulder and pulled me in close. She said, "Donna, you don't need to be strong anymore. It's okay to cry. I'm here."

I could see her. I felt her. I looked into her eyes. In that moment, I saw in my mother the same loving passion for me that I had for my son. I dissolved into uncontrollable tears. That moment in the hospital hallway was pure and true compassion. That moment was not only recognizing her; it was recognizing me. It was love.

The love and trust that I had in my mother that I had hidden behind the locked door of fear were waiting for the moment I could bring it to life. I'm not saying it lasted or that the rage inside of me subsided. But in that moment, when I really looked at her—when I saw her—she saw me.

Einstein has this amazing quote that has long haunted me, that says,

A human being is part of a whole, called by us the "Universe," a part limited in time and space. He experiences himself, his thoughts and feelings, as something separated from the rest—a kind of optical delusion of his consciousness. This delusion is a kind of prison for us, restricting us to our personal desires and to affection for a few persons nearest us. Our task must be to free ourselves from this prison by widening our circles of compassion to embrace all living creatures and the whole of nature in its beauty.

It is the last sentence of this quote that feels imprinted in my entire being. Widening the circle of compassion to embrace all living creatures echoes in my being with the bliss of truth and the pain of fear. For me, embracing all with compassion, at times, has been a tremendous challenge. When I ask myself, who was the first person with whom I felt shame, abandonment, and betrayal, the answer is my mom. She is also the first person to whom I felt love, belonging, and safety.

That first person to whom we feel belonging and that first person whom we perceive abandons us and betrays us has a powerful influence in our thoughts of truth we believe about ourselves. The result for me was a complex and confusing relationship with my mother.

In my own life, in working with my students, in my own therapy, and in coaching, I found that the choice to welcome yourself back to your truth is a powerful choice that can be propelled with key questions.

The questions include:

- Who in your life was that first person to love you?
- Who in your life was that first person to wound you?
- If you imagine that first person who gave you love, security, and belonging, what do you hear them say about you?

- If you imagine that first person who abandoned you, betrayed you, or shamed you, what would that person say about you?

When I did this examination, I discovered that the words were often the ones that I heard in my own head when I was either successful or stuck in anxiety and stress.

The voice that said that I was not good enough or a liar or the voice that said that I could conquer anything were all born of that connection of love or fear. My own voice, the one that said, see her—she's here—that is truth. When we welcome ourselves home and open to the truth that we are complicated and precious beings, the compassion that we can give can transform our lives.

CHAPTER 8 - LISTEN MORE

"The best and most beautiful things in this world cannot be seen or even heard, but must be felt with the heart."
— Helen Keller

When we finally see ourselves and make the choice to want what we want and not hold tight to expecting that wanting to look a certain way, we get closer to the life we want. The same is true in work. If we can see what we want and release our hold on control of what it should look like, we become creative powerhouses. In my life, listening to myself allowed me to listen more and choose to welcome others more fully into my heart. The journey of opening that closed heart of mine began with students.

My mom died on October 30, 2003. In November of 2003, I was named interim principal of the high school where I was a school counselor. The ironic twist of fate is rather humorous. My mom couldn't get her way while she was alive, but in death, she got me right into that limelight. The first day on the job, just one week after burying my mother, I put the key in the lock on the principal's office door and walked in. Standing in my new office was surreal. What happened to the little girl who never wanted to speak to others? What happened to the adult who was so painfully introverted that she would lie to get out of public speaking?

My mother would never know that her shy, introverted daughter was named the principal of a high school, albeit interim principal, which she would have nervously asked me what that meant and if I would always have a job. Or did she know? My mother was always the voice of fear and anxiousness that could easily deflate any ego I held. Perhaps if she had been alive, I wouldn't have had the confidence to say yes to the job but would rather fall into the label of 'shy girl' she had given me with accuracy.

Now, here I was on my first day as an interim principal with no clue what to do. Waiting outside my door was a student and his aunt. The aunt, who was in her twenties, was quietly crying. The young man sat next to her stoically, his arms crossed at his chest. He appeared angry and detached.

They were waiting to request that the principal overturn the student's expulsion and readmit him to the school. I was that principal, and I was nervous. My predecessor had expelled him because of a long list of discipline infractions that could be summarized by saying he was a total nuisance to teachers. He was a kid who disrupted class and pulled pranks on teachers like duct taping all their desk drawers shut. I had heard talk in the teacher's lounge that teachers were relieved he was expelled. It was clear to me that readmitting him would make the teachers angry. It seemed to my newbie principal knowledge that the expulsion followed all the school's protocols.

I awkwardly began the meeting, asking the young man what he had done wrong. His reply, though not shocking, stopped the conversation cold as he said, "I didn't do nuthin." This line of questioning was getting me nowhere fast, and I was convinced the choice of me as interim principal was very unwise. The aunt's tears kept flowing as the young man, who I'll call Mickey, which is not his real name, angrily asked if he could leave the room. I looked him in the eyes, and something in me shifted. I could see myself in his anger. Beyond the anger was fear, and I could feel it. I asked his aunt if I could talk to Mickey alone. She agreed.

I asked him why he was afraid. He paused, looked at me, and said, "What do you care?" The answer shocked me as I expected him to say that he wasn't afraid. I had only asked the question to shift the mood to one of compassion. I wanted him to know that I wanted to help him.

I had assumed that he, like me, was just pretending to not be afraid. I was petrified. I was afraid not only of being the interim principal but of living life without my mother, and as usual, I was afraid of all of life in general. Fear is my constant companion, and pretending I wasn't afraid is one of many lies that came easily to me. What happened during that expulsion appeal meeting would teach me about truth and the power of mercy to find out who I was behind the fear and lies and what my life was meant to be

During the meeting with Mickey, he revealed a tragic story of the unexpected and violent deaths of his mom, dad, and grandma. I kept asking Mickey what he was afraid of and why. Slowly and with caution, he unraveled the beliefs of his fear of abandonment and betrayal. He described our high school as his home and the teachers as the only ones who cared for him. Caring meant any type of attention. I readmitted Mickey. Each day after school, he would stop by my office and talk. My conversations with Mickey ended up helping me as much, if not more, than they helped him. So many of our students were caught in fear of abandonment, betrayal, and shame—just like me.

As principal, each morning, it was my task to do the daily announcements. In the beginning, I would search a prayer book for prayer to start the day. As time went on, I began each day with my intention for the students I grew to love. I wanted to inspire them, to lift them to reach their highest potential. Each day, I called our school a family, and throughout my tenure as principal, we became a family. For Mickey, we were the family that believed in him and gave him chance after chance. And for me, the school became the family that didn't leave me.

My greatest success as a principal was not the academic accomplishments of the students or the fact that I led the development of the very first one-to-one laptop program in a private school in Illinois, or even that I led the school's change of mission from single-gender to a unique co-educational model. My greatest success as principal was consistently listening more than I spoke and choosing to welcome the compassionate me over compliant me. I chose me just as Roger chose me. I wished I had chosen Roger too, but he became the greatest teacher of my life.

Recognizing Love

Love is confusing and a complicatedly paradoxical experience of life. Love has the power to bend a spoon, and love has the power to lift me from drowning. Love also has the power to bring us to our knees. Choosing to want must always involve love. Wanting is love—it is love of something deep within. Love is wanting. I wanted love, and I wanted safety. I had love. I never had safety. No matter how much I tried to hide myself away from love so I could avoid pain and suffering, that darn love found me hiding in the bushes. There are times when the choice of love is not only the best thing to do; it is the only thing you can do.

My brother died. Roger died. I was angry and relieved. The moment I was told Roger had died, I jumped into action without shedding a tear. Things had to get done, and it was easier for me to start running into work than to stop and feel. I needed to handle all the details of the funeral and wake. My dad was in a nursing home, my mother was dead, and my older brother had his own life away from me. I was completely alone, and for me, that was best.

Loving Roger always felt oddly complicated and scary, and now my biggest fear was realized. I remember my mother saying that the doctors told her he would not live long. If I loved him and he died, then what would I do? If I loved him, how could I handle only seeing him on weekends? Trying not to love Roger was just as hard as loving Roger.

At forty, Roger lived in a group home and went to a workshop each day where he packed sporting goods. He got a salary and had a girlfriend. For all appearances of my own guilt, he had a nice life without me.

When the director of his group home called to tell me about the discovery of his testicular cancer, she assured me he would be fine. She asked if I wanted to go with him to an appointment for radiation and treatment. I wanted to do what my mother would do, and I wanted to look like a good sister. I said yes and then tried to figure out how I would balance my busy life as principal with Roger's doctor visits. I also tried to figure out how to get Roger through the long radiation treatments.

Roger loved watching the movie, *The Wizard of Oz*. For three decades, each day, he would watch *The Wizard of Oz* – over and over again. I grew to hate the movie and also love that the movie occupied him. He loved the munchkins, the Lion, the dance down the yellow brick road. He would get scared at the Wizard—every single time. And as soon as Dorothy started to come home, he asked to have the movie play over again.

I bought him a portable DVD player and a copy of the movie to take to the hospital and watch during treatment. I bought him snacks and bottles of water as if he were going on a field trip. I wasn't prepared for what it would be like to have your Down Syndrome brother go through radiation. Roger had always been so easy, so loving, so gentle, and so easily consumed by whatever interested him.

I sat next to Roger as the nurse put the rubber band around his arm to start the IV. He screamed the loudest cry I have ever heard. He jumped up and said, "No, no, no." He was scared. I never saw Roger scared. I started to shake. I didn't know what to do. I tried to comfort him, and he pushed me away. The nurse kept asking for my help. I was completely helpless.

The medical team determined that Roger would need to be sedated for treatment. They couldn't do the treatment in the clinic. He would need to be hospitalized each week to get radiation. I felt I had failed him. Why did he push me away? The little girl in me felt the deepest rejection. I shut down, detached, and went back to work.

Roger's group home caretakers took him to treatment, and I would visit him each weekend after visiting my dad in the nursing home. My dad had been placed on hospice shortly before Roger's diagnosis. Something in me decided to bring Roger to see my dad in the nursing home. I thought I would bring Roger to my dad so he could see him one more time before he died.

The day I picked up Roger, he got into my Jeep with the familiar confidence. He sat next to me and said, "I drive," and laughed. I said, "Nope, I'm driving today." He then said in his familiar voice, "My car." And as always, I replied, "Nope, this one is my car. Roger had very limited verbal expression. He would repeat just a few phrases, with his favorite being, "I quit." He would say, 'I quit' and then laugh with this snide laugh.

We arrived at the nursing home when my dad was taking a nap. Roger and I walked to his room. Roger walked right up to my dad's bed, leaned over him and kissed him hello, saying, "DAD."

The caretakers got my dad up and in his wheelchair. We wheeled him into the dining hall, where lunch was being served. Roger, my dad, and I all sat at a round table. As each resident was wheeled by, Roger would loudly say "HELLO" and wave. Roger sat next to my dad and focused on his face.

I brought my digital camera to get a picture of the two of them together, but it felt rather morose to take a picture of a dying man being visited by his cancer-ridden Down Syndrome son. The camera sat next to me on the table. Days later, when I looked at the images on the camera, I somehow magically captured a 10-second video of Roger, reaching out to my father and comforting him by gently stroking his arm. How did this intellectually deficient, Down Syndrome man know how to soothe his father? Where did that magical compassion come from?

Roger developed an infection and was hospitalized a week later on Easter Sunday. I brought him an Easter basket with his favorite candies and eggs. I went to the room to visit, and his smile was back. He greeted me with his usual "DONNA" and gave me a hug. All was right with the world. He had just been afraid.

When the doctor came in to see Roger, he did a quick exam and asked to speak to me. I started to walk to the hallway, but the doctor just launched into talking. I was sitting on the edge of Roger's bed. The doctor started to describe Roger's infection as if Roger were not two inches from me. Then he said, "I'm sorry, the cancer is everywhere. He's not going to make it."

What? What? Did you just say my brother is going to die right in front of him? What the f**k! How could this be happening? What do I do now? Where do I turn?

The doctor left, and Roger played with the remote control for the television. I kissed him on the forehead and told him I had to go home. He and I were very experienced at leaving each other, but this time was the worst.

Roger went home to his group home, and hospice was called. I met with the hospice intake worker. She looked at me and filled in her forms. I said to her, "You don't remember me, do you?" She paused and said, "This is weird. The name seems familiar." I proceeded to tell her she had met with me just weeks earlier when my father was put on hospice. My brother and father were both on hospice with the same hospice company, and I felt like a number on a chart.

Roger had been moved from the group home where he lived for over a decade to another home that could give him greater care. The hospice company got him a hospital bed and moved his pictures so he could see them. I brought Roger his favorite root beer to distract his pain.

My feelings about Roger are so complex. I carry this disgustingly shameful truth that I didn't like him. Yet, since the age of six, I acted like the "good sister." I taught him to walk. I took him places. I brought him to visit our dying father. I told him I loved him. That was bullshit.

The truth is that having a Down Syndrome brother made me angry, lost, and permanently afraid of betrayal, abandonment and shame. When Roger was born, I lost my father and mother—not literally but definitely emotionally. I know my mother believed it was her fault Roger was "different." I know my father was sad all the time. We all carried a sadness.

When the phone rang at 11:00 p.m., I knew he had died. The director of the group home was crying. Roger was special to them. She kept saying, "I'm sorry."

Roger was dead. My mom wasn't here for me to tell. My dad was alive but gone to the ravage of dementia. I was alone, just like I was in the back seat of that Buick on that dark October night.

I planned the wake and funeral, bringing Roger to my mother's church. I chose the Catholic songs my mother would have liked and the same readings I chose for her funeral. The priest came to the service at the funeral home the day before he would say the Catholic mass. He asked about Roger. He listened to stories of Roger's loving personality and confidence. He heard about Roger's obsession with *The Wizard of Oz* and Dorothy.

Roger didn't have the typical things a priest could put in a eulogy. He did his best to talk about my mother's devotion to Roger and Roger's diligence at workshop. Then the priest paused, looked at me, and began singing "Somewhere Over the Rainbow" A capella. I couldn't breathe.

At the end of the mass, I gave a beautiful eulogy that talked about Roger's ability to make everyone feel loved. I spoke of him constantly saying, "I quit," and laughing. I shared the stories of his Halloween costume as the cowardly Lion in which he was far from cowardly.

I stepped off the altar and felt the coldest emptiness I had ever experienced. Driving home from the cemetery, I glanced over to the passenger seat where Roger sat laughing and saying, "I quit." I shouted out loud, "Why the hell did you constantly say, 'I quit'? What the hell were you quitting anyway? You didn't have anything to quit!"

In that moment, I realized Roger was telling me to quit. He wanted me to quit running, quit hiding and quit thinking I was anything but the sister he loved. I could feel it. I could hear it. I can still hear his voice saying, "I quit."

Roger died on May 23, 2006, just two days before the graduation at the high school where I was principal. I went to work the day after I found out he was dead to get things ready for the graduation I would miss. This graduation was no ordinary graduation. This was Mickey's graduation. I had to tell Mickey that I would not be there for him to give him the handshake and diploma we had worked so hard to get – together.

Mickey was angry. He didn't say the things I wanted him to say that he understood and that it was okay. "No," he said, "that sucks." He was right. It sucked. For four years, Mickey had been why I could manage the challenges of being the first woman principal in an all-boys school and why I wanted to stay. I had done everything possible to help Mickey not get teachers angry and to pass his classes. I think Mickey believed I earned his diploma more than he did. It wasn't true. The universe has an odd way of making things work out for us.

Mickey was able to get his diploma and hugs and handshakes from all the faculty all by himself. He earned that diploma, and it was his moment. I had followed my why and loved him and my brother Roger.

I look back on each annoying thing Roger did and realize I was the one who was annoying. I was so afraid of loving him, I couldn't see the brilliance of all he was here to teach me. His limited phrases, his warm hugs, his laughter, and even his bubble of protection were teaching me about me. He was teaching me there was no choice but to step fully into my own beauty and brilliance and fully into love. No matter how much you try to protect yourself from the suffering of life, love will get you there, and love is the only thing that will save you.

Choose to love your work. Choose to fall head over heels in love with the wanting of work. Be afraid to fail and love when you do not. Choosing love will bend spoons and will make you say, "I quit."

Loving Roger, much better these days, I feel as though I have awakened from a prison of fear. Roger kept giving me the answer in his hugs, smile, and warm embrace. Choose to welcome love into your heart. Yes, your heart will be broken, and yes, it is that same love that will heal you.

CHAPTER 9 - BELONGING TO ALL

"You always had the power, my dear; you just had to learn
it for yourself."
— Glinda, The Good Witch

D efining moments pop into your life when you least
expect them. No matter what business books say,
I'm convinced you cannot design the most
meaningful defining moment. Rather, you just have to
show up and act just like my brother Roger did—as if you
can handle anything that comes your way.

For me, unexpected defining moments have been a
blast. There is something rather odd that comes over me
when the rest of the world is in a panic. I seem to slip into a
state of calm assurance and peace. I got the nickname
"Even Kiel" because of my consistently noteworthy calm. I
do believe having Roger as my brother and watching him
walk into any situation did something to hard wire my brain
for confidence only when everyone else is falling apart.
When I have the raging voices of shame and self-doubt,
there is no even keel.

There is a choice we can make when those defining
moments surface. We can choose to welcome the wisdom
that we know we have, and we can choose to remember
that we are all one universe. For me, those choices have
given me defining moments and the most meaningful
moments of my life. As principal, there are always

opportunities to test your choices. I will forever remember the moment when it felt as if my entire life came together, giving me all I had needed to thrive. I always met with students who asked to see me. This time was different.

This student looked terrified. Most students who came to my office looked petrified. After all, the principal's office is a scary place—even for the principal. Her school counselor accompanied her. I greeted them both with my usual gracious smile. I had become very adept at exuding kindness and keeping any anxiety buried so deeply that no one could see.

Being principal, for me, was a complicated and unpredictable ride. My desire to rescue was often too much, so I would pretend I had all the answers. The principal is supposed to have the answers, and I became great at the pretense. The counselor spoke first and unraveled a story that immediately erased my pretending to be calm. I could feel my body tense, and my heart pound faster. How could this happen under my watch?

I immediately moved closer to her. I reached for her shoulder, wanting to hold her and keep her safe. I desperately needed her to hear me. My entire being wanted to cry for her and with her. The desire to comfort her, to tell her she was alright, to let her know that I would never let anything happen to her became my single thought. I had to let her know I believed her. I had to let her know she was safe. This was personal.

Schools are supposed to be safe havens. They are supposed to be places free from harm for students and adults. Schools are far from safe havens, and even for me, the school became a place of secret violation.

Eight years earlier, as a new faculty member and one of the only women on staff, I was anxious to fit in. When a popular male faculty member welcomed me with kindness, I eagerly accepted his friendship. We would joke around sharing stories. We were buddies. He'd often compliment me, and I liked his affirmation. He often stopped by my office to chat.

On one particular day, he stopped by my office, and things felt odd. He said how great I looked. He moved toward my desk, saying, "Wanna see what you do to me?" I froze. He pulled down his pants. I said nothing. I felt the familiar detachment and emotional distancing I had gained as a skill the first time this happened to me at age four. He left. I never told anyone. I was so filled with shame and fear I pretended it had not happened.

Now, eight years later, I'm no longer his buddy; I am his boss listening to a petrified 15-year-old describe an all too familiar scene where he again is the perpetrator. She cried, "I don't want anything to happen to him; he's my friend." I reassured her. "You did nothing wrong." She began to relay the details. "He was talking to me after school. He's been helping me with boyfriend troubles." I could feel my heart pounding so hard I feared she could hear it. "He said I was beautiful and wanted me to see what I did to him. He pulled down his pants."

How had I let this happen? Had my silent shame contributed to the heinous act? My deep fear that began so many years before had allowed this young woman to be victimized. My image as a powerful, strong woman of integrity who was a decisive and effective principal was all a façade. I hated myself. I had to find justice for this young woman and also find compassion and forgiveness for me. The task felt impossible.

My supervisor asked me if her story was true. How could this beloved teacher do this? I knew the truth. The decision was clear. I fired him immediately. The faculty were enraged. Students were upset. I had stepped into my integrity and felt the shaming of a culture that denies things we cannot handle.

I was ordered by the school attorney to never share the details of the perpetrator's acts to protect him and the school's reputation. I complied. I went on with my work and kept moving. It is amazing how time moves forward, and we forget terrible things. School moved on, and so did I.

The challenges of high schools are never-ending. Declining enrollment and financial strain were an ongoing battle for me. Each year, I had to lay off teachers to make the budget work. Two months after I had to secretly let go of the faculty member accused of molesting the student, we held a faculty meeting designed to boost morale. Tensions were high as we faced yet another year of layoffs.

To deal with the emotional toll of the principalship and to deal with the sexual abuse of our student, I distanced myself from everything. I dove deeply into work with a laser-like focus on getting tasks done. I let go of any support service that might have made my job less daunting. I was doing the master schedule, running programs to make extra money, and handling all the after-school events. I was a non-human functional machine.

The best part of the faculty meeting would be that I didn't have to run it. An alumnus who was a leadership expert and brilliant facilitator had agreed to serve as the leader of the meeting. The goal of the meeting was to rebuild the faculty unity—or so I thought. What ensued during the meeting was a fear-driven attack of my leadership and me.

The former principal who hired me launched the first missile. He stood and spoke emphatically about how he came to school each day afraid he was going to be fired for no reason. He talked about the school leadership (me) not living the mission of the school. Some faculty countered his remarks, but the damage was done. Those faculty who were often performing marginally joined in the attack. They said decisions were made in secret and treasured faculty were dismissed without cause.

After the meeting, the alumni who facilitated met with me and the president of the school. He was a brilliant man who was a neurosurgeon and renowned expert in organizational management. His first words were that the culture of the school was toxic. He was extremely supportive of me and said his advice was to eliminate those faculty who clearly had limited capacity to act as mature professionals. His words, while affirming, did little to help mend my battered and bloody soul. I hated myself for causing such pain in these people. I was angry.

The choices disappeared along with my soul. I had lost myself to the heinous acts of a man who chose to abuse a young girl. I was that young girl. Anger and sorrow make choices disappear.

Mercy

There are moments in a woman's life in which all of the cultural norms collide with the truth. I was a principal who led a school of over eight hundred students and one hundred faculty to be the first fully one-to-one laptop Catholic school in the state in 2003. I was the principal who changed the mission of a school from single-gender to uniquely co-educational with a men's and women's leadership academy. I was the first woman principal of the school who was supervised by a man and who was hired by a dominantly male board of directors. On my staff were five former principals of the school. Each of the former principals had either been asked to step down or had chosen to step down for reasons that were obvious. Those former principals were not my employees who often had a great deal of advice for me.

I was a woman, I was a leader, and in 2011, after eight successful years as principal, I was in trouble. I was living a life that I detested. I didn't know who was calling the shots and every day felt like a roller coaster ride of responding to the wants and needs of whoever was at the controls. I worked long, sixteen-hour days and wasn't sleeping. I had lost a tremendous amount of weight, and my five-foot-five frame was holding up only 117 pounds. During my tenure as principal, my mother had died, my brother got cancer, my dad slipped into dementia, then my brother died, and my father died. My term as principal had been one hell of a ride.

In June of 2011, at the end of that school year, my evaluation from the president of the school was exceptional. He said he had nothing I needed to improve upon, and so his recommendation was that I finally finish my doctorate. During my evaluation meeting, he leaned in and said, "You are far better than this place—get the damn doctorate."

I had consumed myself with work as I usually did to hide from my feelings and the truth of what was happening to me. I moved way too fast through my days to even notice that I was slowly falling apart. The sexual abuse incident with the young student followed by the faculty meeting that criticized my leadership were arrows to my heart that joined the arrows of my own personal life that was a disastrous situation of my selfish decisions.

School had ended in May, and by June, I was in full swing of creating our own online program for summer school. We were trying to make money at summer school, and so I was busy creating the curriculum myself. If we had an online summer school, I wouldn't have to pay teachers, and the kids would still be able to get quality credit. The program was set to start the last week of June, and I was frantically trying to do this while also creating a master schedule. The president of the school asked me if I had some time to meet with him. We scheduled a meeting for the end of the day on a Friday. When Friday came, I was woefully behind in getting things done, and so I asked if we could cancel. He agreed, and we rescheduled for the following week.

The president and I had an incredibly strong relationship that was often more like father and daughter. He would give me life advice, and in turn, I would create for him successful programs that kept the struggling school going. I had no doubt of his belief in my skill or his confidence in my leadership. He had a joke going that he often went through his life with WWDD as his mantra, standing for 'What would Donna do?'

When I went into his office and sat across his desk, we exchanged pleasantries about the summer and family. He seemed uncomfortable and distracted, which was unusual for him. He began saying, "I don't know how to say this." I felt my heart immediately sink and flashed back to the final meeting with the principal at the all-girls school.

I never imagined he would apologetically say he needed to give me a message that was difficult on behalf of the board. He was careful to say this was not his message. He did not agree.

I had a stellar record, school planning was in full swing, and I had a signed contract for the next school year. Heat filled my head and face, and it was hard to hear. He said there had been meetings between the director of the board and several faculties. He made sure to say several and not all faculty. He said the board director went behind his back and asked the faculty about my leadership. He went on to say how he was so angry and felt disrespected that the board director usurped his leadership. He threw that board director under the bus.

I didn't ask any questions. I didn't need to. I chose to welcome me home. The moment I walked away from the school, it was as if I had been freed from prison. I had constructed my own prison of silence, shame, and denial. The students of the school, Mickey, the young girl who bravely shared her story of sexual assault, and each of the students I met have been my greatest teachers of grace.

The young student who came into my office petrified to speak of the coach she loved as the perpetrator of abuse left my office as a woman of courage and integrity. She risked all she knew to speak her truth with grace and dignity. It was years after my resignation that I even realized that I had fired the coach for sexual abuse just three months before I was asked to resign. It took several years for me to see the truth that I chose to resign long before the president and board asked me.

You do not need to change a thing. You do not need to keep searching, seeking, and believing there is some answer that exists outside that will tell you the truth. You are exactly what the world needs as there is only one you. This is true of me, and it is true of you. I know, with certainty, that you are a brilliant and needed light in this world because I am you, and you are me. We are 'the all' we need to choose.

CHAPTER 10 - PERFECTLY TRUE

"No matter how difficult and painful it may be, nothing
sounds as good to the soul as the truth."

— Martha Beck

C hoosing anything, whether it is to **watch** your
wisdom, to **want**, to **welcome**, or to **wonder**,
requires just two things—truth and love. After
choosing to leave my first principalship, I very reluctantly
signed on to be the principal of a small rural school fifty
miles from my home. I ran away from anything that
reminded me of what I perceived were my mistakes, and of
the life that I felt I didn't fit any longer.

The principalship in this public school became a source
of healing and renewal that I could never have imagined. I
thought I was running away, but my choice to be a
principal again, to pick myself up and show myself and the
world that I was a strong, creative, and inspirational leader,
gave me the most unexpected beginning of growth and
transformation.

Deep within me, there was a calling to help others own
their truth. I was so busy calling myself a failure and a liar
that I couldn't hear that I was a creative, loving, and
compassionate woman of truth. When we let go of shame,
the freedom of integrity is born, and with it, we step into
the glorious peace of living our highest and truest potential.

Honoring You

During the senate judiciary hearings for Supreme Court Justice nominee Brett Kavanaugh in which Dr. Christine Blasey Ford testified that Mr. Kavanaugh had sexually assaulted her, I became enraged and felt more anxious than I ever have. The Friday the hearings ended, I attended a Martha Beck workshop in Boone, North Carolina. Martha, a sexual abuse survivor herself, began her talk by saying how much the hearings bothered her and the trauma they awakened. She asked if anyone had anything they needed to say or if they had any questions. She asked who in the audience was troubled. I raised my hand as high as it would go. Another woman spoke of her abuse and how facing her perpetrator was the most difficult thing she had ever done.

I quickly raised my hand, which is odd for me since most of the time, I work hard to not be seen in situations like this. Martha stood directly in front of me with the most compassionate glance and called on me to talk. I told her and the audience of hundreds of people that I felt like a coward and failure because I had never shared the abuse that happened to me. Martha then gave me the greatest gift of compassion. She stepped down, came closer and said, stop. She went on to say you did what you needed to thrive and survive. She shared that she didn't share her abuse until after she had two best-selling books and established life. She told me I was not a coward and that I, too, deserved the compassion and mercy I felt for Dr. Ford. She told me it was okay to protect myself. It was the most compassionate choice I could make. There are times in your life when you are ready to step into truth and times when the unexpected truth calls you to stay, be okay, be loving and kind to yourself.

Deep within you is the truth that requires no choice. In the authentic moments of empathy and mercy is the choiceless truth that you are a complex and precious person who is love. You are the only choice you ever need to make.

EPILOGUE

It is time to stop searching, seeking, and recreating our lives. Rather, it is time to celebrate the incredibly perfect version of you that exists right now. Now I am not saying stop trying to grow and learn. What I am saying is that the most important thing for any of us to do is to love ourselves deeply. It is when we love ourselves deeply that we can love others. To love ourselves deeply, we must pause, go inside, and seek our own truth. It is in living true that you discover you are complete, whole, and perfect just as you are.

As Mary Oliver asks, "What are you going to do with your one wild and precious life?" My hope for you is that you live your truest life with the realization that you are precious, glorious, and needed. You are worthy because you are here. You are loved. You are lovable. You are the truth of all that we need.

There is a wonderful Eastern spiritual teaching that is referred to as the Splendor of Recognition. The teaching says that when God creates a person, God implants a small part of God in each of us. When we meet each other, it is our greatest gift to see the goodness in the other as that is the goodness in us. My wish for you is that your life is grounded in living your truth and in seeing the goodness that is in you reflected in each of those around you. You are perfect, whole, and completed as you live true!

Made in the USA
Monee, IL
14 June 2022

97990646R00075